Wiping the War Paint off the Lens

VISIBLE EVIDENCE

Edited by Michael Renov, Faye Ginsburg, and Jane Gaines

Public confidence in the "real" is everywhere in decline. The Visible Evidence series offers a forum for the in-depth consideration of the representation of the real, with books that engage issues bearing upon questions of cultural and historical representation, and that forward the work of challenging prevailing notions of the "documentary tradition" and of nonfiction culture more generally.

VISIBLE EVIDENCE, VOLUME 10

Wiping the War Paint off the Lens

Native American Film and Video

Beverly R. Singer

Foreword by Robert Warrior

 University of Minnesota Press

Minneapolis

London

Published by the University of Minnesota Press
111 Third Avenue South, Suite 290
Minneapolis, MN 55401-2520
http://www.upress.umn.edu

Library of Congress Cataloging-in-Publication Data

Singer, Beverly R.
   Wiping the war paint off the lens : Native American film and video / Beverly R. Singer ; foreword by Robert Warrior.
      p.   cm. — (Visible evidence ; v. 10)
   Includes bibliographical references and index.
   ISBN 0-8166-3160-3 (alk. paper) — ISBN 0-8166-3161-1 (pbk. : alk. paper)
      1. American Indians in motion pictures.   2. American Indians in the motion picture industry—United States.   I. Title.   II. Series
 ⌄ PN1995.9.I 48 S56 2001
      791.43'6520397—dc21
                                                            2001001939

Printed in the United States of America on acid-free paper

The University of Minnesota is an equal-opportunity educator and employer.

12 11 10 09 08 07 06 05 04 03 02 01   10 9 8 7 6 5 4 3 2 1

Contents

ROBERT WARRIOR

Foreword

In the summer of 1998, I sat in a Tempe, Arizona, movie theater packed with several hundred people from the Native American Journalists Association's annual meeting for a sneak preview of Chris Eyre's breakthrough film *Smoke Signals*. Most of the people at that screening were American Indian teenagers. The film was much anticipated among those who have charted the progress of Native American film, so I watched eagerly.

Though far from being a perfect film, *Smoke Signals* features impressive direction, some wonderful performances, and masterful use of a small budget. But I became just as interested in watching the audience watching the film as I was in the film itself. The young people I saw the film with were enthralled, seeing reasonable facsimiles of themselves and their lives on the big screen—most of them, for the first time.

I remember thinking that it was like they were watching *Star Wars*. And insofar as that group of American Indian young people was seeing something on a movie screen they had not seen before, it was. But rather than special effects and a galaxy far, far away, what those young people in Tempe and thousands of filmgoers that summer saw was pretty much new to them: American Indian actors playing American Indian characters, saying words written by American Indian screenwriters, and following direction from an American Indian director.

Star Wars, of course, was not the first space opera, nor was it the first really good one. Neither was *Smoke Signals* the first, or the best, American Indian foray into film. And that, needless to say, is what Beverly Singer's *Wiping the War Paint off the Lens* is about. In the chapters that follow, Singer tells the story of how American Indian film and video makers have been taking up the challenges of telling stories to be seen on screen rather than read on the page or heard within tribal traditions.

The tradition of Native filmmaking that Singer presents here speaks volumes about the larger context of American Indians in the history of American film. The relationship of American Indians to movies and movie making is deep and long and rarely positive. From its early days, the movie industry has capitalized on American Indian characters and stories. One of Thomas Alva Edison's first moving pictures was called *Sioux Ghost Dance* (1894) and played into America's fascination with the American Indian religious movement of the same name that a few years previously had swept the West, ending in tragedy with the massacre at Wounded Knee in 1890.

That massacre itself later became the subject of a feature film when William "Buffalo Bill" Cody traveled to the Dakotas to re-create what happened at Wounded Knee. Buffalo Bill gathered Sioux men and women, many of them survivors of the massacre, and captured the staged event in a film that has unfortunately—or perhaps fortunately, given the macabre nature of the project—been lost to history. Other Hollywood films, most notably *Nanook of the North* (1922) and *The Silent Enemy* (1930), attempted faithful recreations of nonmilitary American Indian life.

But such attempts at realism have been the exception rather than the rule. Instead, directors from D. W. Griffith to Kevin Costner have banked on a mix of romanticized images of American Indians as noble, stoic, bloodthirsty, and defiant. As Comanche writer Paul Chaat Smith argues, "The movies loom so large for Indians because they have defined our self-image as well as told the entire planet how we live, look, scream, and kill." And, until recently, the main contribution American Indians could make to the production of these images has been in playing bit parts and being extras. Yet, at the same time, Smith says, "If it's true that Indians have been deeply involved in the movie business, it's also true that those films aren't really about Indians in the first place."[1]

The standard American Indian reaction to this situation over the past three decades has been to complain about the lack of sensitivity of filmmakers to the true story of American Indians on this continent. When Sasheen Little Feather took the stage at the Academy Awards in 1973 to reject Marlon Brando's Oscar for *Last Tango in Paris* (1973), it was to protest the entire history of how Indians had fared in Hollywood. Such complaints have been followed up with demands for more opportunities for American Indian screenwriters, directors, and producers. Singer covers the same ground as these earlier critiques, taking us from the days when American Indian actors worked as exploited extras and bit players to more recent times when accomplished players like Graham Greene and Tantoo Cardinal have played important roles in major films. But rather than rail against the unwillingness of those within the film industry to change their attitudes toward American Indians, Singer sets off in another direction.

However marvelous American Indian performers have been and are, Singer reminds us that control of the images coming out of films rests with writers, directors, and producers. Singer, thus, is interested in those moments when Native filmmakers have managed to gain control of the camera and the rest of the filmmaking process. Her major focus is on the past three decades, when a discernible body of film and video, with titles numbering in the thousands, directed and produced by American Indian people, has emerged.

Throughout, she demonstrates that American Indian control of the camera and the process is crucial if American Indian people are to be more than the objects captured and emulsified on film. Singer, as someone who has been a participant in this exciting history, offers a unique blend of knowledge and insights as she shows the strides American Indian directors have made in learning the craft of filmmaking over the past two decades.

Those strides in American Indian film and video making have covered the ground from the handful of short feature student projects by American Indians who have gone through the American Film Institute or New York University to the more ambitious attempts at full-length features and experimental films. The story as she presents it is far from over—indeed, it seems to be only now coming into its own.

American Indian film and video making, though, not only have happened in the broader context of American film, but also are interwoven within the larger context of American Indian life. If the nineteenth century casts its shadow across American Indian history through war and disease, this past century has been one in which American Indian people have had to learn how to both adapt and survive at the same time. Lagging behind in every socioeconomic category from educational attainment to per capita income, Indian people have lived on the margins of American consciousness, typically neglected while others are attended to, normally forgotten in the litany of America's successes and failures.

In the midst of invisibility, though, the twentieth century also saw a remarkable resilience among American Indian people. Asserting their humanity in the face of a world blinded to the problems modernity has brought to the Indian world, and asserting a continued belief in Native sovereignty as the best way of bringing American Indian solutions to American Indian problems, Indian people have managed to come into this new century and millennium having defeated the notion of the idea of their inevitable vanishing. Along the way, those who have become doctors, lawyers, novelists, astronauts, Olympic athletes, and other sorts of professionals have overcome stereotypes and lack of opportunity to pave the way for new possibilities.

Filmmakers have done the same as they have taken up the task of demonstrating their ability to do excellent work at the highest level of a complex, modern art. Yet, like contemporary American Indian novelists and poets, they can also do much more. That is, contemporary American Indian filmmakers regularly present their audiences with some of the deepest existential questions that modern indigenous people face, questions that often have to do with how it is that history, tradition, culture, and identity move forward into the American Indian world as it changes.

Shelly Niro's *Honey Moccasin* (1998) does just that sort of thing in its exploration of how a Native community can continue in the face of the theft of the clothing and other objects it uses in its dances. Victor Masayesva's work, which includes extensive use of narrative in the Hopi language and experimental film techniques, brings to the fore issues of where Native aesthetics fit into larger questions of film and its meanings. Even Arlene Bowman's disturbing *Navajo Talking Picture* (1986), an example Singer discusses at length, in which a Navajo filmmaker attempts to capture her extremely reluctant grandmother on film, highlights central issues of identity and cultural change.

These films and others represent much more profound attempts at exploring the parameters of these issues than anything Hollywood has produced. Characters in American Indian films and videos do not participate in the cliché of "walking in two worlds" (unless the filmmaker wants to be ironic). The moving image's three dimensions lend itself instead to a more complex version of these and other critical questions.

Programs such as the Sundance Institute have actively supported American Indian filmmaking, and the number of scripts in various stages of development is growing by leaps and bounds. The pool of acting talent is becoming deeper, as is the pool of Native people who can work behind the camera as assistant producers, dolly grips, best boys, and boom operators. The advent of digital technology will open the world of filmmaking even more.

Singer, then, offers us a serious look at American Indian filmmaking midstream. The discussion she frames has much to tell us about both general and specific issues in film studies and in American Indian studies. And what makes her discussion especially valuable is that she takes us beyond the topic of all those images that Smith points out are not really about American Indians anyway. *Wiping the War Paint off the Lens* cuts to the all-important set of questions about what American Indian people, who have lived through such a dramatic period of change over the past two centuries, have to say about themselves through the medium of film. More than that, she lets us know that American Indian filmmaking has a vital history made by an impressive array of film professionals who have paved the way for what is happening today and what can happen in the future.

Clearly, American Indian filmmakers work at their craft because they love it and because they love the potential it holds for bringing new aspects of what it has meant and means to be Indian in America to life. As with any serious enterprise, these filmmakers need serious, informed audiences who can join in the discussion. Beverly Singer, both as one of those committed filmmakers and as a student and scholar of the overall field, has taken important steps toward leading that discussion.

Prologue in Three Parts

Tsikumu is a special mountain to the people from Santa Clara Pueblo, my community of origin. It sits among the Jemez Mountains, which are part of the Rocky Mountains, in north central New Mexico. I remember annual hikes to Tsikumu peak in my youth with my parents and four younger siblings. We hiked there to thank the Spirits for our well-being and to petition for rain to bless our community. Our prayers were always answered. Tsikumu is a divine presence in my memory as old as Creation.

A memorable leader from Santo Domingo Pueblo named Mateo Aragon passed to the spirit world in 1968. He advocated on behalf of Indian youth so that they would receive greater benefit from education. At one particular conference concerning a curriculum on Southwest history, he remarked: "You teach our Indian students history, but everything is about the white man."[1] I am guided by Aragon's courage and thank his spirit of advocacy that came from his heart.

Watching *Smoke Signals* (1998) at a West Hollywood theater in the summer of 1998 was a new movie-going experience for me. I went to see the film because it was written by Sherman Alexie (Spokane/Coeur d'Alene) and directed by Chris Eyre (Cheyenne/Arapaho). I am ready to see more films made by my people. I hope another century won't go by before we get to enjoy at a local theater another film made by Native people.

Acknowledgments

The inspiration for this project was derived from the artistry and conviction of the following Native American filmmakers who deserve special acknowledgment and many thanks: Victor Masayesva Jr., Sandra Osawa, Ava Hamilton, Ruby Sooktis, Darrell Robes Kipp, Joe Fisher, Arlene Bowman, Bob Hicks, Loretta Todd, Gary Farmer, Chris Eyre, Randy Redroad, Shelly Niro, and Alanis Obomsawin.

Jane Caputi deserves special mention for having encouraged my interest to complete a study about Native Americans in film when she was a faculty member with the American Studies Department at the University of New Mexico. As chair of my dissertation committee, she gave me the support to remain true to the original spirit of my study. Additionally, grateful acknowledgment is reserved for professors Marta Weigle, chair of the Department of Anthropology, University of New Mexico; Philip May, Department of Sociology, University of New Mexico; and Kathryn Shanley, Department of English, Cornell University, who read and reread my final study with healthy criticism and support.

The American Studies Department at the University of New Mexico deserves recognition. American Studies permits the synthesis of several academic disciplines that enabled me to combine Native American culture, history, and filmmaking, which is the foundation for what I have written here.

Arlene Hirschfelder, Shannon Rothenberger, and George Leong contributed in unique ways to the completion of the study. They are gifted writers, mentors, and friends who taught me what is important about life and the pursuit of scholarship.

While rewriting my study for publication, two of the most important people in my life passed to the spirit world, my mother, Bertha M. Singer, and my grandmother, Florence N. Singer. They are with me now as I draw on their strength. My father, James, continues to teach me the value of community and education, as do my siblings Norman, Tanya, Dwayne, and Camille, along with their children, who fill me with light and love to keep on with the work that I truly enjoy.

I have derived knowledge from many individuals and their encouragement endures. I ask forgiveness from many others who are not on this short list: Faye Ginsburg, Jennifer Moore, Nancy Sauro, Donald Wylie, Yvonne Wakim, Sue Milus, Lotus Do Brooks, Norbert Hill Jr., Barbara Feith, Connie Maffei, Juanita Espinoza, Pegi Vail, Sally Berger, Rich Tamayo, Daniel Hart, Karen Stone, Karen LeSage Stone, Elizabeth Weatherford, Emelia Seubert, Fiona Wilson, Erica Wortham, Ted Jojola, Darrell Waldron, Jake Swamp, Lynn Reyer, and Theodora Yoshikami.

I acknowledge my ancestors' spiritual foundation on which I continually rely to guide me.

Introduction

Thinking Indian Thoughts

One of the most important issues facing American Indians concerns the question of identity: What is an Indian? The historical misrepresentation of "Indians" has been outside of tribal control and perpetuated by American cultural, political, academic, and social institutions that promote, produce, and communicate information to the public. Indians have been misrepresented in art, history, science, literature, popular films, and by the press in the news, on radio, and on television. The earliest stereotypes associating Indians with being savage, naked, and heathen were established with the foundation of America and determined by two factors: religious intolerance for cultural and spiritual differences leading to the destruction of Native cultures, and rejection of Indian cultures as relevant subject matter by traditional historians in the writing of U.S. history.[1]

The demise of the Indian presence, accompanied by the westward movement of pioneers and viewed as a major American victory, was the result of a struggle among whites for economic, political, social, and religious independence. The ideology of Manifest Destiny was the propaganda used against Indians to justify our extermination. Noted writer D'Arcy McNickle (Métis,[2] enrolled by the Flathead Tribe) recalls that "Until the third decade of the present century Indian policy was rooted in the assumption that the Indians would disappear."[3] The enduring perception of Indians as an enemy pending extinction cleared the way for anyone to create stereotypes of Indians and to exclude any serious treatment or study of us. Challenged by this inimical history, this book builds on scholarship of and interpretation by Native people who have worked to share the totality of the American story in our images.

This study grew out of my interest in tribal storytelling as a transfer of cultural information and in its intersection with the growth of filmmaking by Native Americans. Over the last twenty years Native Americans have made some outstanding films and videos. My discussion of these films and videos draws on my experiences as both a Native American and a video maker. As Native American filmmakers, we have faced many struggles in our attempts to make films, competing for limited resources and struggling to overcome popular stereotypes that present us as unintelligent and refer to us in the past tense rather than as people who inhabit the present. What really matters to us is that we be able to tell our own stories in whatever form we choose. This is not to say that whites cannot tell a good Native story, but until very recently whites—to the exclusion of Native people—have been the only people given the necessary support and recognition by society to tell Native stories in the medium of film.

The chance to remedy the lack of literature about telling our own stories is deeply connected to being self-determined as an Indian. It is part of a social movement that I call "cultural sovereignty," which involves trusting in the older ways and adapting them to our lives in the present. These rights and traditions include defending our birthrights as agreed to by treaties, speaking our tribal languages, practicing ancestral methods of food harvesting such as spearfishing and whale hunting, gathering medicinal herbs, and using animals and birds for ceremonial purposes.

Our films and videos are helping to reconnect us with very old relationships and traditions. Native American filmmaking transmits beliefs and feelings that help revive storytelling and restore the old foundation. By making our own films, however, Native Americans threaten traditional practices of Hollywood filmmakers, who often advanced their careers by creating distorted and dishonest images of "Indians." In my own filmmaking experiences, I have felt at times as though I were trespassing into the most white-entrenched profession.

Chapter 1 highlights current views held by Native people concerning identity and the expression of it. Chapter 2 looks at the early recruitment of Indians to perform in movies and provides a summary of the studies related to the stereotypes created about Indians. Chapter 3 provides historical background showing how the way was prepared for me and many other Native people to have the opportunities to create films. Chapter 4 surveys the origins of Native film and video production in the United States and Canada. Chapter 5 outlines a cultural framework of storytelling and applies it to six films by Native filmmakers. In the conclusion, I consider more recent efforts by Native Americans to take control of the institutions and alliances that support film production as well as pointing out areas where much more effort is needed.

An essential element of my work is that I avoid using traditional film categories to discuss Native film and video. Terms that identify films as "avant-garde," "documentary," or "ethnographic" limit the understanding

and information contained in Native films and videos, and they are not natural categories within our experience. By avoiding comparison of American
Indian cultures with dominant white Euro-American culture terms, this
study advances the dialogue about the influence of Native culture on filmmaking. Native social structure and belief systems are different from the
Euro-Western "scientific method" of obtaining data to solve a problem.
Whatever the label—Aboriginal, American Indian, Native American—we
are tired of being referred to as the "Indian problem." So, my discussion
begins with an "Indian solution."

The oral tradition is fundamental to understanding Native film and
video and how we experience truth, impart knowledge, share information,
and laugh.[4] Traditional Native American storytelling practices and oral histories are a key source of our recovery of our authentic identity. Leslie
Marmon Silko (Laguna) believes that the ability to tell stories is a way of life
for Pueblo people. She believes that older stories and newer stories belong
to the same creative source that keeps the people together. Furthermore, she
states that "the Origin story functions basically as a maker of our identity:
with the story, we know who we are."[5] Simon Ortiz (Acoma) writes that in
his experience the power of stories—such as the origin stories shared among
the Pueblo people—is that words take hold of a storyteller and "go their own
way." Story making at this instant becomes the language of experience, sensation, history, and imagination.[6] Today's storytellers continue the practice
of an art that is traced back countless generations and safeguard that the
stories are being carried into the future. Paula Gunn Allen (Laguna/Sioux/
Lebanese), in her study of American Indian oral tradition, states that

> The oral tradition is more than a record of a people's culture. It is the creative
> source of their collective and individual selves. When that wellspring of iden-
> tity is tampered with, the sense of self is also tampered with. . . . The oral tra-
> dition is a living body. It is in continuous flux, which enables it to accommo-
> date itself to the real circumstances of a people's lives. That is its strength, but
> it is also its weakness, for when a people finds itself living within a racist, class-
> ist, and sexist reality, the oral tradition will reflect those values and will thus
> shape the people's consciousness . . . and they will incorporate that change,
> hardly noticing the shift.[7]

That the oral tradition is a continually evolving process is apparent in
Aboriginal and Native American films and videos, which are extensions of
the past in our current lives. Additionally, stories and their telling may also
connect us to the universe of medicine—of paranormal or sacred power.[8]
Storytellers are highly valued because they have the power to heal the spirit.[9]
One of the reasons for making films is to heal the ruptures of the past, rec-
ognizing that such healing is up to the viewer.

TAOS TALKING PICTURE FESTIVAL   TAOS, NEW MEXICO, USA APRIL 6-9, 1995

Jonathan Warm Day, "A Night for Song and Stories." 1995 Taos Talking Picture Festival, Taos, New Mexico. Copublishers Jonathan Warm Day, Lawrence D. Egan, and Steven Villalobos. Copyright Martin-John Graphics, Denver, March 1995. Reproduced by permission of the artist.

Poet Luci Tapahonso (Navajo) explains how Navajo stories are viewed as being true by members of her tribe: "A Navajo audience is unlikely to doubt the storyteller's assertion that the events related did indeed occur. It is also understood that the stories or songs do not 'belong' to the teller, but that her or his role is that of a transmitter."[10] Native filmmakers are "transmitters," too! The integrity associated with storytelling or filmmaking in this context remains sincere.

Today, as in the past, Native people are exploited by others for information. This treatment has increased Native peoples' desire not to see that practice continued with their work today. Fred Nahwoosky, independent consultant to Native cultural organizations, points out: "Indian people offer explanations on Indian terms and present culture directly from tradition bearers, so that it cannot be misinterpreted by outside scholars. This is a strategy for eliminating stereotypes, validating the beliefs and practices of native groups, and retaining intellectual property rights to cultural patrimony."[11] It is my intention in this book to present our story of filmmaking on Indian terms.

[1] *Bringing Home Film and Video Making*

▶

Determining Our Self-identity

In 1989, Charlene Teters (Spokane) attended a University of Illinois basketball game with her son and daughter. After watching a half-time performance by the university mascot named Chief Illiniwek, her life was radically altered. The mascot was a student dressed in Plains Indian regalia wearing an eagle feather headdress and "Indian" war paint who pranced around the arena to ersatz "Indian tom-tom" music played by the university band. Teters, a graduate student at Illinois at the time, recalls seeing her children slump in their seats as the befeathered mascot led a crowd of cheering fans. She was acutely aware that her own and her children's Indian heritage was violated by the performance of Chief Illiniwek.

Teters questioned administrators at the University of Illinois about the "Indian" mascot, noting that it was offensive to her American Indian beliefs and practices. University officials were defensive and claimed the mascot was a long-standing tradition meant to honor historical Indians. Teters continued to question the mascot issue and began a personal protest of it, standing on campus with a sign that read "Indians are human beings, not mascots." But instead of receiving support for her efforts to raise student awareness about the unsuitability of having a mascot that misrepresents Indians, she was seen as a threat. The sports fans who upheld the use of the mascot were remarkably hostile in their resistance to eliminate the practice. As news spread of her protest, her criticism produced a backlash of attacks against her and her family from university students, alumni, local businesses, and state officials.[1] Teters's persistence brought national attention to the mascot issue as other universities and high schools with mascots named after Indians began debating their continued use of them. The University of Illinois Regents voted to retain their mascot tradition with support from the state of Illinois. A bill was passed to protect the mascot, although Illinois governor Jim Edgar later vetoed it.

In 1992, Teters graduated with an M.F.A. from the University of Illinois and vowed to continue her opposition to "the Chief." She is a founding board member of the National Coalition on Racism in Sports and the Media. In 1998, Teters was featured by ABC News with Peter Jennings as the "Person of the Week" for her advocacy against racism targeting American Indians.

Teters's history of public challenge to the commercial exploitation of American Indians is the subject of the nationally televised documentary *In Whose Honor?* by Jay Rosenstein, in which she states, "Our people paid with their very lives to keep what we have left. And we have to honor that sacrifice."[2] Her spirit of advocacy is projected in all aspects of her life; she explains:

> My teaching, art, and revolutionary activities have centered around restoring my distorted birth rights, not only for myself but for others. Tragically, many Indian people must become involved in the struggle to reclaim themselves. Beyond victimization there must be recovery. Recovery must come from within; all that can be done by those on the outside is to get out of the way, to correct their own mis-education.[3]

The revolutionary artist role with which Teters identifies is not unique, nor is the Indian mascot tradition the only "mis-education" that Indians need to recover from and redress.

Another important form of "mis-education" about Indians is their negative portrayal by Hollywood. Victor Masayesva Jr., a Hopi filmmaker, responded to a hundred years of Hollywood Indian movie portrayals in *Imagining Indians* (1992).[4] Masayesva features the personal experiences of Native people who have participated in Hollywood productions from the late 1930s to the 1990s and exposes their manipulation by Hollywood filmmakers, comparing their behavior to early Indian agents who took land from Indians for white settlement. Masayesva translates this historical practice and applies it to white filmmakers who take aspects of Indian culture and use their own interpretation of the culture to make their films.

In *Imagining Indians,* Masayesva views the portrayal of "imagined Indians" found in Hollywood movies and the manufacture of Indian art objects as parallel activities that contribute to the commodification and dehumanization of Native people. One scene in the film takes place at the annual event known as the "Santa Fe Indian Market," where the production of Indian art is strictly commercial and driven by collectors who don't care if a set of Indian kachinas are exactly alike. (Kachinas are in the domain of the spirit world, acknowledged, in particular, by the Hopi, who craft multifarious representations of them such as the Long Hairs, Corn Maidens, and Ogres. Prior to the tourist trade, these were carved from wood, painted, and used to teach children about the many different kachinas. In the tourist trade they are known as "kachina dolls," which today are mass-produced and are exactly alike, such as those shown by collectors in Masayesva's video at the Indian Market.) A collector interviewed at the market admits, "We're totally saturated and there's no space to lay these rugs on the floor, and there's no set place to house these dolls [holds up a box of Navajo dolls], but this becomes a disease, one just keeps buying, buying, buying." This replication of popular images of Indians for commercial purposes— whether in films or other forms of culture—contributes to a loss of respect for culture, confused identity, and weakened beliefs about what it means to be a Native American. In a further demonstration of unraveling popular images of Indians, Masayesva turns to his own community of Hopi Indians, who are viewed as a peacefully united people with sacrosanct beliefs. In 1994, a Hollywood film crew sought to film at the Hopi reservation in a place revered by a group of elders who opposed any filming there. However, the elected Hopi tribal government accepted a payment in exchange for allowing the filming, and the matter was dismissed.

While Masayesva relied on historical parallels and real-life events to expose some of the effects on Indians of the years of stereotyping, Sherman Alexie (Spokane/Coeur d'Alene) confronted the stereotypes by turning them on their heads and getting people to laugh with Indians rather than at them. His serialized novel *The Lone Ranger and Tonto Fistfight in Heaven* (1993) became the basis for his screenplay for *Smoke Signals* (1998, Miramax), directed by Chris Eyre (Cheyenne/Arapaho). The film is about two young men, Victor and Thomas, who grow up in the shadow of a family tragedy that sets up the undercurrent of their uneven relationship at a reservation in the Northwest. The plot focuses on Victor, the recent death of Victor's father, and the journey the young men take to revisit their past while recovering the father's remains. Alexie's writings creatively explore the range of experiences found in any community that shares like values and traditions. His stories are not an exhibition of Native or Indian culture, but a rendering of the feelings of Natives today.

Over twenty years ago Vine Deloria Jr., one of the patriarchs of American Indian scholarship, identified two contradictory belief systems— traditional and Western European—that Indians live with. This contradiction, he said, functioned as a continual source of conflict for Indians about their identity. Deloria wrote:

No matter how well an Indian may become, he or she always suspects that Western culture is not an adequate representation of reality.

Life therefore becomes a schizophrenic balancing act wherein one holds that the creation, migration, and ceremonial stories of the tribe are true and that the Western European view of the world is also true. Obviously this situation is impossible, although just how this became impossible remains a mystery to most Indians. The trick is somehow to relate what one feels to what one is taught to think.[5]

Deloria's perceptions remain pertinent today, as evidenced by Bob Jones (Seneca), a twenty-five-year-old ironworker in Buffalo, New York. In 1993, a magazine produced by the Discovery Channel interviewed Jones on his views about being a young Native American. He said that the "white man's education" he received left him feeling unsure of who he was as an Indian. A major concern for Jones was the lack of cultural knowledge among younger Indians, which he believes creates serious doubts about being Indian. "What you have are a bunch of modern-day Indians who like to be Indians but don't know how to be. It's a tough thing trying to mix old-time culture and tradition with modern-day politics. . . . If you know who you are then you're unlimited as to where you want to go. . . . I believe that, so that's what I'm trying to figure out, who the hell I am."[6] Jones and tens of thousands of Indians like him have realized that they must search for their true identity and then fight to keep it. Jones's statements about Indian identity echo Deloria's of twenty years earlier: "the representation of Indian people should be a post of heavy responsibility. . . . It takes a lot of hard work to raise an entire group to a new conception of themselves."[7]

In my search for words to simplify my point about culture and identity, Debra Lynn White Plume, who lives on the Pine Ridge Indian Reservation, says them for me: "I would say that there are two revolving themes that live in what I write: resistance and celebration. In our daily lives the most beautiful form of all is actually LIVING the philosophy, history, culture and ways of our Lakota people!"[8] In this book I illuminate the work of Native American filmmakers who have both celebrated their cultures and resisted the effects of centuries of assimilation.

▶

Producing and Directing Ourselves

The decade of the nineties produced an abundance of Native media about the changes that took place in the twenty years since Deloria called for Indian self-representation. Filmmaking, print journalism, radio programming, and the Internet are compiling our individual stories into the larger story of Native survival and continuance. The result is a growing sense of unity about our place in history and the role we have in helping to shape the future.

The special attention that I give to Native Americans' own filmmaking is intended to demonstrate how film and video visualize the healing from the ruptures of our history related to colonialism, disease, and cultural loss.[9] Our identity as filmmakers also helps to reverse the devastating effects of assimilationist educational policies that coerced a sense of inferiority in us.[10] Therefore, my use of "filmmaker" is conscientiously applied throughout my discussion to promote our participation as filmmakers in America, although for the majority of us, the only means of producing work is in video.

My work can be seen as an example of what anthropologist and media scholar Faye Ginsburg calls "indigenous media," which she defines as a means for indigenous people to negotiate self-identity and representations of social, cultural, and political themes that transcend boundaries of time, space, and even language.[11] Victor Masayesva Jr. refers to indigenous media as a journey for "tribal people to consider and reflect on the White man's most seductive and reductive invention for conception and representation which we have today: film and television." Masayesva was the artistic director for the Imagining Indians: Native American Film and Video Festival in 1994, an unusual opportunity for Native people to produce a film festival that he described "as the start of Native American initiatives to shape the models of our self-awareness."[12]

All filmmaking is a risk-taking venture, but too often the rationale given by funding organizations for rejecting Native American film proposals is that they are not as good as other proposals and that as filmmakers we lack experience. The underlying attitude is that we as Native filmmakers are unconventional in our approach to filmmaking and too often personally invested to a fault in wanting to make films about our people. But it is only through our participation in filmmaking that we can help to create mutual understanding and respect.

The comprehension of culture as it relates to Native filmmaking comes from the storytelling approach that always pays homage to the past but is not suspended there. The currency of our experience is energized by self-expression that validates and comforts our desire to participate in the world of ideas. The process also works to detox our own ingrained stereotypes of Indians that block our creativity. Creating films and other visual art is a dynamic within Native American life that, according to art curator and scholar Rick Hill (Tuscarora), "comes from our ancestors to which we are bound to add our own distinctive (traditional) patterns."[13] Hill's reference to art as part of life also affirms Masayesva's perspective that filmmaking is not a separate activity but an integral one.

As a general rule Hollywood "Indian" movies are set in late nineteenth-century America. This time frame, according to Navajo filmmaker Arlene Bowman, is a problem when "the average American cannot accept Native Americans' present realities and always look at Indians in the past; I am not putting the past down but we are for real and living today."[14] Bowman, who has a degree in motion pictures and television from the University of California at Los Angeles and has produced two major films, has not been able to access mainstream media in part because the accomplishments of Native American filmmakers are not recognized as valid if they do not conform to expectations of how Indians look and act in movies.[15]

Following the enormous popularity and financial success of *Dances with Wolves* (1990), several new film and television projects were announced, including Kevin Costner's own TIG Productions documentary titled *500 Nations,* which was shown on prime-time CBS-TV in 1995.

Two years before, in 1993, Ted Turner held a press conference to announce his Native American media initiative. This was at the height of the controversy over his ownership of the Atlanta Braves baseball team and his endorsement of the "tomahawk chop" by Braves fans, an arm gesture that is offensive to Native Americans. Turner's project, the *Native American Series,* was comprised of TV documentaries, a book, and several historical dramatic films, which were broadcast on Turner Network Television.

Both the Costner and Turner projects were seen by Native filmmakers and writers as hopeful opportunities to be hired as writers, producers, and directors and to promote new images and current views held by Native peoples. I was disappointed, after watching only portions of the Costner and Turner programs, to see that they were merely recycled images of historical photographs of Indians taken by white photographers with emphasis on the social problems facing Indians.

Phil Lucas (Choctaw) was hired to direct one of the documentary programs, and Hanay Geiogamah (Kiowa/Delaware) was listed as a cowriter for the *Native American Series,* but it was obvious that they did not have decision-making power, given the revival of stereotyped images of Indians in many of the programs. Ruth Denny, a journalist for the *Circle,* an independent Native newspaper published in Minnesota, wrote an editorial about the Costner and Turner projects after she received no response to her request for information from their production companies for how Native Americans could apply for jobs on these productions. In hindsight, her criticism was justified when she wrote, "Native Americans do not need any more Kevin Costners, Billy Jacks, and John Waynes. . . . The need for the

Indian expert is over."[16] Denny is referring to America's history of Indian experts who are white and male.

Directing, producing, and writing for films and television are professional careers not typically associated with Native people, but there have been some refreshing changes in Hollywood of late. A new generation of Aboriginal and Native American actors have appeared in title roles in movies that feature Indians. The nineties have seen a number of Native Americans pursuing acting careers in film and television in Canada and the United States, including Adam Beach (Ojibwe) and Evan Adams (Cree), who were in *Smoke Signals*; Irene Bedard (Inupiat/Cree), who was in the title role of *Lakota Woman* (1994), was the voice of Pocahontas in the Disney production of *Pocahontas* (1995), and was also in *Smoke Signals*. More seasoned performers who also need to be acknowledged include Tantoo Cardinal (Métis/Cree), whose credits began in 1975 with projects in Canada and who was highly acclaimed in the United States after her appearance in *Dances with Wolves*; Gary Farmer (Cayuga), who became a Native cult hero for his role in *Powwow Highway* (1989) and was in *Smoke Signals*; Graham Greene (Oneida), who received an Oscar nomination for his performance in *Dances with Wolves*; Steve Reevis (Blackfeet), who had a unique role in *Fargo* (1996) and was featured in the independent film *Follow Me Home* (1997), directed by Peter Bratt; Wes Studi (Cherokee), who portrayed Geronimo in the contemporary remake of *Geronimo* (1993), a role he earned after his performances in the most recent rendition of *The Last of the Mohicans* (1992) and *Dances with Wolves*; Sheila Tousey (Menominee), who was cast in a key role in *Thunderheart* (1992) and was featured in the HBO film *Grand Avenue* (1996), written by Greg Sarris (Coastal Miwok).

Although most films and videos produced and directed by Native people document actual life stories, some are narrative films. Native fiction reveals insights familiar to Native people through characters acted by Native people who identify with these roles as belonging to their peoples' experiences. An early one of these was *Return of the Country* (1983), written and directed by Bob Hicks (Creek/Seminole) as his graduate thesis film in directing at the American Film Institute in Los Angeles. The film's plot revises all historical assumptions by having Indians discover America and establish a Bureau of Caucasian Affairs, a twist on the actual Bureau of Indian Affairs established by the U.S. federal government. Hicks used his creative license to reverse the dynamics of white and Indian relationships throughout *Return of the Country* by having white children abandon English, shed their European-style dress, and turn away from Christianity.

Another early narrative film is *Harold of Orange* (1984),[17] written by

Still from *It Starts with a Whisper* (1993), written, directed, and produced by Shelly Niro and Anna Gronau. Photograph courtesy of Shelly Niro.

Gerald Vizenor (Ojibwe). The film is about Harold, an ingenious Indian from the reservation, who applies for a grant to open coffeehouses on the reservation. Harold and his friends, nicknamed "the warriors of Orange," travel to the city in a school bus to present their proposal to a foundation. Their visit, which is an adventure for Harold and his buddies and an education for the whites at the foundation, is very humorous to audiences who know the underlying themes associated with the paternalistic attitudes toward the Indians shown in *Harold of Orange,* such as the myth that all Indians are alcoholics and the insensitive display of ancestral Indian remains in museums. *The Honor of All* (1989), directed by Phil Lucas (Choctaw), is a reenactment of the debilitating effects of alcoholism in an Aboriginal community named Alkali Lake and tells the story of the cultural and spiritual recovery of the entire community. *Tenacity* (1994), directed by Chris Eyre (Cheyenne/Arapaho), was completed while Eyre was enrolled in the M.F.A. filmmaking program at New York University. The film opens with two young Indian boys about ten years old playing combat on a rural road and their encounter with two white males in a truck who have been partying. *It Starts with a Whisper* (1993), codirected by Shelley Niro (Quinte Bay Mohawk) and Anna Gronau, is about a serious young Aboriginal woman who is unsure of herself and is taken for a joyride by her amusing spirit aunts. *Haircuts Hurt* (1993), directed by Randy Redroad (Cherokee), is a short film about a Native woman's decision to have her young son's hair cut at a "redneck" (bigoted) barbershop.

As this sample of films shows, Native American filmmakers have many stories to tell about themselves and their culture. If they can be given opportunities to share their work, we just need to sit back, watch, and listen.

[2] *The War-Painted Years*

▶

Indian Stock and Hollywood

The prominence of stereotypes of American Indians in early Hollywood westerns sacrificed the humanity of Native people. The western movie genre, an outgrowth of the dime novels that were published up through the early 1900s, exaggerated the Western frontier as a confrontation between good and evil, and characterized it as civilized white man against wild Indian savages and outlaws.[1] To make matters worse, early Hollywood filmmakers often relied on the labor of real Indian actors for portrayals of "savage Indians."

The hiring of real Indians by Hollywood movie producers to appear in their movies was the result of the participation of Indians in Wild West shows, beginning with Buffalo Bill's Wild West Show, which opened in Omaha, Nebraska, on May 17, 1883, and was organized by William F. Cody. Cody was featured in dime novels and used his legendary popularity as a Pony Express rider, scout, and "Indian fighter" to establish himself as an entertainer. He recruited actual Pawnee, Sioux, Cheyenne, and Arapaho Indians to reenact battles for movies while actual battles continued in their homeland. Others began organizing their versions of Wild West shows and followed Cody's lead by using different tribal Indians to portray Plains Indians.[2]

The new century brought an end to Wild West shows, their popularity replaced by Hollywood movies that celebrated white civilization subduing Indian "savagery." Anti-Indian sentiment was strong, encouraged by President Theodore Roosevelt (1901–1908), who openly expressed his contempt for American Indians and promoted Manifest Destiny as an ideology justifying westward expansion: "The Indians never had any real title to the soil.

Indians attack a white man in the film *Flaming Frontiers* (1938). Photograph courtesy of Hulton Getty, London.

This great continent could not have been kept as nothing but a game preserve for squalid savages."[3] The views held by Roosevelt and other entrepreneurs of the period were fueled by their interests in obtaining Indian lands and resources, a goal that motivated the public abasement of Indians, particularly in American popular culture.[4]

Native Americans who previously had worked in Wild West shows were natural performers in front of movie cameras. A Winnebago Indian named James Young Deer, for example, performed in Wild West shows at the turn of the century and made his transition to movies in 1903. His movie credits include a feature role in D. W. Griffith's *The Mended Lute* (1909), which established him as the first Native person to become a "movie actor." Young Deer married a fellow Winnebago actress named Red Wing, and by 1909 they were well-known personalities in Hollywood.[5]

Young Deer's experience with staging battles for Wild West shows earned him the opportunity to be hired as a movie director for Pathé Frères, a French film company. He also served as general manager for the company's Pathé West Coast Studio. The movies directed by Young Deer include *Cheyenne Brave* (1910), *The Yaqui Girl* (1911), *Lieutenant Scott's Narrow Escape* (n.d.), and *Red Deer's Devotion* (n.d.). Young Deer's directing career was apparently short-lived, because in 1916 he returned to acting and started an acting school.[6] The films directed by Young Deer fit the narrowly defined genre of the period: displays of Indian attacks against rugged Western pioneers with simplistic fictive plots emphasizing male heroism and unrequited love.

The Chickasaw heritage of Edwin Carewe may have advanced his friendship with the writer Jack London, who introduced Carewe to his brother Finis Fox, a Hollywood screenwriter. Carewe was hired in Hollywood and started his career as a director when he borrowed the Fox family's collection of Indian artifacts to make the movie *The Trail of the Shadow* (1917).[7] His career coincided with talkies, motion picture sound, and his production of *Ramona* (1928), starring Delores del Rio, was one of the first movies with sound. Carewe hired the young del Rio for the leading role, launching her well-known Hollywood acting career.[8]

Edward Carewe and James Young Deer are anomalies in the social history of Hollywood movie making. But because they are identified as Native Americans, and in spite of their short careers in Hollywood's formative years, they are important to the Native American filmmaking story. They proved their ability to direct successful commercial movies alongside the major director of the period, D. W. Griffith, who directed over thirty "Indian" movies.[9]

▶───────────────────────────────────────

War-Painted Years

In 1910, a vaudeville performer named Thomas Ince began working in Hollywood and quickly rose to the rank of producer and movie director.[10] At the time, westerns were becoming increasingly profitable, and in 1911 Ince arranged for a group of about twenty-five Sioux from the Pine Ridge Reservation to reenact battles for his westerns. As was the case in the Wild West shows, many of the Indians selected by Ince had fought real battles as young men.[11] Known in Hollywood as the "Inceville Sioux," they had a negative reputation as a result of their abuse of alcohol both off and on the movie set. The Sioux Indians who were imported to Hollywood by Thomas Ince were boarded at a ranch with beds in the animal stalls, and most meals were provided on the film set. They received a small sum working as film extras. The exact amount of their pay is not documented, but a week's pay was enough for many Indian extras to get drunk at local saloons, and Ince was called by bartenders to deal with his "wards" who were "disturbing the peace."[12] It was said that their drinking provoked them to carry out their battle scenes with realistic fervor.

Ernest A. Dench was an outspoken movie critic who was opposed to real Indians performing in Hollywood movies. In 1915, Dench wrote an essay titled "The Dangers of Employing Redskins as Movie Actors," concerning the reports that Indian actors indulged in too much realism with their clubs and tomahawks and endangered white actors, in effect reliving their "savage days." Dench also exposed to the public the threat imposed by the use of real bullets during filming. He decried the salaries earned by Indians working in Hollywood movies, pointing out their aberrant use of "firewater" (Dench's term) and tobacco. Dench concluded that whites should portray Indians not only because they were better actors, but also because "to act as an Indian is the easiest thing possible for the Redskin is practically motionless."[13]

Sadly, Dench's criticisms were most likely misdirected. It is hard to imagine that the Sioux Indians turned to alcohol by themselves without someone in Hollywood getting it for them until they learned more English. Furthermore, Ince had accepted full responsibility for the Sioux from Pine Ridge when he took them to Hollywood, having received permission from an Indian agent. Ince's westerns were enormously successful, and within a short time he was one of the first movie directors to build a mansion in Hollywood.[14] The Inceville Sioux, on the other hand, disappeared from history.

A deviation from the Hollywood studio system occurred in the 1920s, the height of popularity for Hollywood westerns. The first independent filmmaker to work outside of Hollywood was an explorer named Robert Flaherty, who began filming in northern Quebec and produced *Nanook of the North* (1922). The film, based on the life of Allakarialak, an Itkivimuit hunter, and his family, represents Flaherty's personal encounter with Inuit Natives in the 1900s.[15]

Nanook of the North was the first independently produced film to have a national theatrical release. Flaherty's example was the foundation of documentary film. Anecdotes about Flaherty's attempt to distribute the film through a Hollywood studio illustrate the power of movie executives whose primary motive is commercial profit. One studio executive noted, "It was a film that just couldn't be shown to the public."[16] He considered the film too realistic, and it conflicted with images of warring Indians in the Plains with which Americans executives at the time were comfortable. Originally funded by the French film company Revillon Frères, Pathé, the film company that had hired James Young Deer, became the distributor for *Nanook of the North*. The film was a commercial and critical success, and even today it is said to stand in a class by itself.[17]

Another film that strove to portray the reality of Indian lives at the time was *The Silent Enemy* (1930). A millionaire explorer-naturalist named

William Burden produced the silent film, and it was directed by H. P. "Daddy" Carver. The film was a dramatization of an Ojibwe encampment struggling to avoid starvation by hunting caribou. To achieve authenticity, the filming was completed in the Temagami Forest of northern Ontario and featured a mostly Native cast. *The Silent Enemy* opened in May 1930 at the Broadway Criterion Theater in New York City to an enthusiastic, privileged audience that included the surnames Morgan, Roosevelt, Vanderbilt, and Whitney.[18] Despite positive reviews, the movie failed at the box office.[19] The primary reason for the movie's failure is that it could not compete with talkies.[20]

A young Penobscot woman named Molly Spotted Elk had a key role in *The Silent Enemy.* The role became a stepping-stone for her career as an international performing artist following the movie's release. According to Spotted Elk, the producer and director of *The Silent Enemy* regularly sought the advice of selected members of the cast, and "the picture grew out of the actual life experience of our players." Although the intent of the movie makers was for accuracy of the Indian portrayals, Spotted Elk believed it was unfortunately misdirected, overemphasizing material culture, clothing, tools, and housing at the expense of capturing the essential relationships and attitudes of the Native people in their struggle to survive. Even with the producer's desire for accuracy, he couldn't escape the influence of the Hollywood Indian. For example, Spotted Elk related that a chief named Yellow Robe provides an introduction to the film, wearing full Plains Indian regalia rather than Ojibwe clothing.

With the introduction of location filming, hundreds of Native people became more accessible to Hollywood directors interested in enhancing a sense of realism in their westerns. Charles Sooktis, a Cheyenne elder, recalled his experience working as an extra for the film *The Plainsman* (1936), directed by Cecil B. DeMille, with Gary Cooper in the lead role. Sooktis and other Cheyenne were hired for the location shooting in Montana. In one action scene, Sooktis says they were told to charge their horses across the river. Unbeknownst to the Indian actors, a wire was strung across the river to trip their horses. Sooktis recalls that the wire did escalate the drama, but he also recalls that while the Indians were in the river the white hero and his men were filmed behind a barricade shooting at the "Indians," their feet firmly on dry ground. According to Sooktis, some of the Indian extras lied to DeMille about being real chiefs so that they could play the role in films, including the actor who portrayed Yellow Hand. Yellow Hand was thrown from his horse into the water during the river scene, and although he was not injured, his regalia and feathered headdress were soaked and drooping over his face. Unfazed by his humorous appearance,

Wesley Ruggles (1889–1972) (left), the Hollywood film director, seen here with Humming Bird (Chickasaw) and her husband, Louis Brave. They advised on Indian matters in the RKO *Cimarron*, directed by Ruggles in 1930. Photograph courtesy of Hulton Getty, London.

he would not allow anyone else to portray the chief because he wanted to be famous.[21]

By 1936, opportunities for Indian actors were declining rapidly following the Great Depression and an increase of white actors taking Indian roles in the movies. An Indian Actors Association was organized in response to their decreased opportunities for movie work. The Indian Actors Association attempted to gain memberships to the Screen Actors Guild (SAG), but the seventy-five Indian members were unsuccessful. The majority of Indian actors had been film extras with nonspeaking roles, which did not qualify them for SAG membership. Conveniently for SAG, an organization of white actors, the Indian actors did not have legal representation to protect themselves from unscrupulous film producers who had brought Indians to Hollywood as extras at the outset.[22]

In 1940, Indians who had worked as extras in early westerns found themselves with fewer opportunities for working in Hollywood films due to the flooded market of B-westerns. Their diminished status as Indian actors included the group's leader Chief Thunder Cloud (Ottawa) from Canada, an aging actor whose credibility among his peers stemmed from his portrayal of Geronimo in the 1939 movie, and for being the original voice of Tonto on the *Lone Ranger* radio broadcast from 1936 to 1939.[23] Thunder Cloud led the group in filing a petition with the Bureau of Indian Affairs in Washington, D.C., for federal recognition as a tribe of "Indians who worked in films." Their petition was rejected by the BIA. The federal recognition process is a legally binding relationship between an Indian tribe and the federal government. An Indian tribe must prove and retrace its ancestry and history to a specific land base in the United States and demonstrate a form of self-governance as a tribe over an extended period of time.

The attempt by the Indians in Hollywood to be recognized by the federal government as a tribe was mentioned in the *New York Herald Tribune,* which referred to the Indian actors as the "DeMille Indians."[24] The Indian actors at this time were caught in the post-Depression era and literally hungry. Given the desperate nature of their petition to be recognized as a tribe of Indians in Hollywood, they must have felt like a tribal entity given life on the streets of Los Angeles with no practical employment skills except for acting in films.

As the popularity of western movies waned in the mid-1940s, lower-budget films produced extremely negative images of wild, bloodthirsty "Indians." These films appropriated bizarre "Indian" costumes coupled with story lines that positioned American Indians as outcasts in America.[25] Continuing to portray Indians attacking white Americans, as it has throughout its history, Hollywood's effective use of Manifest Destiny also served the wartime fervor in the 1940s. Movies glorifying General Custer as a martyr to the cause of Manifest Destiny were especially popular.[26] The declining interest in westerns and the increasingly negative portrayals of Indians are underscored by *My Darling Clementine* (1946), John Ford's last film for Twentieth Century Fox, which portrays "Indians" as segregated outcasts of society who deserve to be killed.[27] During World War II, Native Americans had served admirably, for example, Navajo soldiers during World War II protected America by using the Navajo language to transmit secret military codes that were never broken by the enemy.[28] But movie audiences were repeatedly shown wild "Indians" threatening white society.[29] Rather than a threat to white society, Native Americans had used their culture and skills to protect it.

By the late 1950s and into the 1960s, Hollywood studios changed course and developed plots focused on personal relations between "Indians" and whites. Combined with this change in story approach, white actors replaced Indians in the majority of roles, although there were a few exceptions. Chief Dan George appeared in *Little Big Man* as Old Lodge Skins, a role that won him a New York Film Critics Award in 1970 as best supporting actor, at the age of seventy-one.[30]

Two renowned Native American actors who have since returned to the spirit world are Harold Preston Smith and Will Sampson. Smith, a Mohawk from Canada, was born in 1912 and was better known by his stage name, Jay Silverheels. He became a television legend portraying Tonto in the serial TV program *The Lone Ranger*, from September 1949 to September 1957. The role of Tonto is considered ignoble because the character represented a stereotype of the submissive and silent Indian in the presence of whites. But Silverheels acted to counteract the negative images of Indians, claiming that he "hated the Indians in the movies. They were always so cruel."[31] Silverheels, who died in 1980, worked behind the scenes in Hollywood to correct negative images of Indians. He was a member of the board of directors for the Screen Actors Guild and served as chairman of the Minority Board for SAG. He also helped organize the Native American Workshop in Hollywood. His work is a striking reminder that many Native people are drawn to movie careers to change the perception of "Indians."

Will Sampson, a Muscogee Creek from Oklahoma, was born in 1933. He rose to prominence as an actor after costarring with Jack Nicholson in *One Flew Over the Cuckoo's Nest* (1975), which won an Oscar for best picture. This major Hollywood movie was not about "Indians," but a narrative about real lives. Sampson's character, Chief Bromden, befriends Nicholson's character in a mental institution. Sampson broke the "silent Indian" stereotype and spoke as a human being. He opened the way to the kind of roles that Native American actors seek. Sampson also helped organize the American Indian Registry for the Performing Arts, a group in Hollywood that sought to continue the struggle for healthier opportunities for Native Americans in the film industry. After his death in 1988, the Registry dedicated a special issue of its *Talent Directory* to Sampson's memory and observed their respect for him: "We Have Now Lit the Pipe for You."[32]

Sampson and Silverheels based their professional careers on acting. But founding members and leaders of the American Indian Movement (AIM) have also had acting roles in contemporary Hollywood movies. AIM co-founder Dennis Banks (Anishinaabe) appeared in *War Party* (1989), *The Last of the Mohicans* (1992), and *Thunderheart* (1992). Former AIM leader Russell Means (Lakota) has several movie credits including *The Last of the Mohicans* (1992), *Natural Born Killers*, *Wagons East*, *Wind Runner*, and a voice credit in Disney's animated *Pocahontas* (1995). John Trudell (Santee Sioux), also a former AIM leader, appeared in *Thunderheart* and as a recording performance artist. Their acting performances in the 1990s are the antithesis of their original message as AIM leaders who were caustically critical of Hollywood movie portrayals of Indians. Their roles are based on

John Big Tree, one of the American Indians in a scene from the film *She Wore a Yellow Ribbon* (1949). Photograph courtesy of Hulton Getty, London.

the old stereotypes of Indians; the plot of each movie remains rooted in the defeat of Indians in American history. Their personal decisions to participate in Hollywood movies continue the tradition begun by Sitting Bull, Red Cloud, Black Elk, Chief Joseph, and Geronimo when they were engaged by William F. Cody to perform in his shows nearly a century ago. Buffalo Bill's Wild West Show exploited these Indian leaders in humiliating demonstrations that reenacted the cultural genocide they had fought to prevent. We now hope to remember them as historic Native leaders, not actors.

[3] *Toward Independence*

▶

Inspired Change

The Civil Rights movement and Black and Chicano activism in the late sixties and early seventies were influential for Native Americans, inspiring many to generate an indigenous version of these movements. Widespread and raging poverty had contributed to the debilitating spread of alcoholism and anomie on Indian reservations and urban enclaves as well. The "war on poverty" programs initiated by the Johnson administration between 1964 and 1968 were designed to provide grants to improve the living conditions of all poor in the United States. The Bureau of Indian Affairs and the Indian Health Service were the federal agencies responsible for overseeing the health and welfare of Indians on reservations more specifically. Indoor running water, sewer systems, and primary health care were serious issues for Indians, along with the need for better education. The BIA also had oversight in negotiating lease agreements on behalf of tribes with energy corporations seeking to extract raw minerals, oil, and gas from Native lands in exchange for bargain-priced royalty payments to Native American governments.[1]

Vine Deloria Jr. was director of the National Congress of American Indians between 1964 and 1967 and recalls this period as a time of change in the political landscape for Indians: "The government officials knew that if they were unreasonable or did not make concessions to the tribal officials, they would be confronted by activists who sought even more radical change than did the tribal councils."[2] He also observed that "the ceremonials of the Plains tribes were filled to overflowing with Indians, many of them urban activists who had come to join in the revitalization of Indian cultures."[3] Deloria's early critical assessment of events taking place among

Indians just prior to the 1970s provides an important historical perspective on the changes we are undergoing presently.

Wilma Mankiller, former principal chief of the Cherokee Nation of Oklahoma, recalls the period leading up to the 1970s in her autobiography. She and others also began to feel the time had arrived for Native people to change their behavior: "For too many years, most native people had lived as if they were being held hostage in a land their ancestors had cherished for eons before the Europeans ever came ashore."[4]

A first effort in that direction occurred in 1962, when the Institute of American Indian Arts (IAIA) was established by the Bureau of Indian Affairs in Santa Fe, New Mexico. The Institute marked a new philosophy for educating Indians, proclaiming that "traditional expressions in the arts by American Indians can be extended . . . [and] enriched in its present state by techniques that consider well the universal forces of creativity, contemporary demands, and respect for cultural difference."[5] The school attracted wide attention in its formative years as an extraordinary institution and is the birthplace of many professional artists of Indian descent. The Institute was the earliest educational program operated by the Bureau of Indian Affairs that accepted the responsibility to teach Native American art and culture at the high school or postsecondary level.

In 1967, a special Senate investigation and review of American Indian education was initiated by Senator Robert F. Kennedy, who unfortunately was murdered prior to its completion. However, his brother, Senator Edward M. Kennedy, continued to conduct hearings at Indian reservations and visited several primary schools with the intent of formulating new policies concerning Indian education. The final report presented to Congress was titled "Indian Education: A National Tragedy—A National Challenge" and contained sixty recommendations for changes to improve education for Indian youth.[6] The primary problem identified in the report was an absence of relevant Indian history and culture studies. It called for stronger community and parent participation in school policy making.

As a result of these calls for improved Indian education, in 1968 the Navajo Nation founded Navajo Community College (since renamed Dine College). It was the first institution for higher learning established by a Native nation and located on an Indian reservation. Nineteen other American Indian community colleges operated by Indian tribes were established by 1970, a figure that grew to thirty-one by the year 2000.

The timing of the report on Indian education coincided with a growing consciousness among Native people. The Bureau of Indian Affairs recognized the growing unrest of American Indians but did nothing to support the call for change. The BIA was criticized and opposed by Native people, who held the agency accountable for failing to enforce and protect legally sanctioned Indian rights. The Puyallup and Yakima Nations in the Northwest began exercising their fishing rights despite opposition by game and fish departments in Washington and Oregon. In 1969, Alcatraz Island in San Francisco Bay was the site of a revolutionary occupation by a collective calling themselves "Indians of All Tribes." Their goal was to build a cultural center on Alcatraz Island.[7]

In the Midwest, the American Indian Movement (AIM) was organized in Minneapolis in 1968, provoking a national political dialogue with the federal government. The group's armed challenge to the federal government at Wounded Knee, South Dakota, in 1973 brought international media attention to AIM leaders. American Indians were enrolled in American colleges in greater numbers than ever before, and yet many left college temporarily to join the protests led by the American Indian Movement. AIM rallies were held throughout the country; for example, AIM leader Russell Means came to the Institute of American Indian Arts in 1973. The Bureau of Indian Affairs did not sanction Means on the campus,[8] but his impact was widely felt. Many students at IAIA began to question their role as artists and that of the school. Some interrupted their careers, while others redirected their art by creating work that represented the body politic.

Other more widespread changes in Indian Country included a revival of cultural and ceremonial practices and new resolve for improving tribal economies. Native people had always understood their strength was culturally derived, but were finally able to begin expressing it openly. Through the 1970s many felt the power of Native culture. It had not disappeared; it had been suppressed by the federal government. The focus on Indian issues led to a shift in public attention that helped produce changes in federal policies, laying the groundwork for creating economic opportunities on Indian reservations that opened the way for gaming, i.e., casino operations. History has a way of leveling the playing field in certain areas of Native life, but the purest measure of change took place in Native hearts. We began to define and esteem ourselves as we embraced our cultural heritage and ancestral practices.

In 1976, art historian and curator Ralph T. Coe received a request from the Arts Council of Great Britain to curate an exhibition titled "Sacred Circles: Two Thousand Years of North American Indian Art." The exhibit opened in London and traveled to the Nelson Gallery of Art in Kansas City in 1977. The success of the exhibition, which was highly acclaimed by critics and purveyors of Indian art, convinced Coe to organize a second exhibition, "Lost and Found Traditions: Native American Art 1965–1985." The opportunity for travel to Native communities brought Coe in direct contact with artists who were working with traditional ideas to create new works of fine art. Coe states in the exhibition catalog, "In many ways not that much has changed between the Indian world I visited and that of long ago. The scenario is drastically different, but not the fundamental underlying patterns [of culture]."[9]

▶

Details from History: The Indian Melting Pot

"Citizens of the United States should not have their rights limited by separate governments within the United States,"[10] professed Senator Slade Gorton of Washington in his congressional move to eliminate American Indian self-governance. Among the first laws of the land enacted by the United States were signed legal agreements with Indian nations, in some cases treaties signed in the 1770s. Since that time, the relationship between Indian nations or tribes and the United States has been legally bound. Senator Gorton's attempt in 1998 to annul such laws are ill-intentioned, as they implicate that Indians are divisive elements in American society because they have special rights.

The misrepresentation of Indian legal history has long been used by politicians to abolish federal protection for lands Indian tribes retain in their possession. In 1953, Congressman William Henry Harrison from Wyoming introduced Concurrent House Resolution 108, articulating a policy to begin the termination of the federal trust responsibility of Indian tribes.[11] The impact of H.R. 108 was the inception of a program to relocate Indians from the reservation to cities where they were promised assistance in developing new skills and improving their living conditions by assimilating into mainstream American life. From the late fifties through the early sixties, the BIA managed the Relocation Program and actively persuaded thirty thousand Native people to leave their reservations.[12]

The Relocation Program did not officially end until 1980. According to American Indian studies professor Michelene Fixico, the program was "also an effort at making Indians a part of the *melting pot*." In hindsight, the program actually led to the "creation of Indian ghettos in the cities," such as those in Chicago, Denver, Los Angeles, Minneapolis, and San Francisco.[13]

Chief Wilma Mankiller recalls her firsthand experience with the Relocation Program in San Francisco:

> Large numbers of Native Americans began to move en masse from reservations and ancestral lands to targeted metropolitan areas in anticipation of receiving

job training, education, and a new place to live. My own family experienced the pain of United States government relocation. The year was 1956. It was one month before my eleventh birthday. That was when the time came for our Trail of Tears.[14]

The relocation experiment brought suffering to many Indian families, but fortunately it failed to achieve its intended purposes, according to Mankiller:

> Termination certainly never even came close to liberating anyone. If anything, those policies had only increased the misfortune and despair among native people. Whether they would admit it or not, government officials also must have been disappointed. Although thousands of American Indians had been relocated, the Relocation Act's goal of abolishing ties to tribal lands was never realized—thank goodness.[15]

Adam Fortunate Eagle was born in 1929 at the Red Lake Chippewa Reservation in Minnesota. He sees the elimination of the reservation system as a long-term goal of the federal government so that the government can gain control of the natural resources that belong to Indian tribes. Fortunate Eagle says:

> Without any Indian lands to administer, the BIA, the oldest bureau in the federal government, could be shut down. This rearrangement would allow the large corporate structure which operated in concert with the federal government to quickly grab up the natural resources. The last vestige of Indian country would disappear into the history books, which could then proudly proclaim that the American Indian has finally become fully assimilated into the mainstream of American society.[16]

Fortunate Eagle's perspective has history to back him up. The problems associated with federal Indian administration have long been known. Lewis Meriam, writing in 1928, meticulously documented many of them. Among the most severe policies drafted for Indians, he says,

> was that of educating Indian children in boarding schools far from their homes, taking them from their parents when small and keeping them away until parents and children become strangers to each other. The theory was once held that the problem of the race could be solved by educating the children, not to return to the reservation, but to be absorbed one by one into the white population.[17]

Throughout history individual members in Congress carried forward the philosophy to suppress Native sovereignty. Prior centuries had already shown that outlawing Indians' religious freedom—including banning dances and ceremonies on the basis of appearing pagan or immoral—did not ensure cultural genocide.[18] Treaty rights and promises made by the federal government to Indians in exchange for Indians' land, property, and rights to worship were continually threatened. Writer Simon Ortiz (Acoma) describes how the non-Indian world also desired that Indians join the mainstream:

> I went away from my home and family to go to boarding school, first in Santa Fe then in Albuquerque. This was in the 1950s, and this had been the case for the past half century for Indians: we had to leave home in order to become truly American by joining the mainstream. On top of this was termination, a US government policy which dictated that Indians sever their relationship to the federal government and remove themselves from their lands and go to American cities for jobs and education. It was an era which bespoke the intent of US public policy that Indians were no longer to be Indians.[19]

By 1960, Native people knew their lives would never be the same as their ancestors. There was no turning back to the old traditional forms of governance either. Traditionally appointed chiefs had been dead for some time and spiritual leaders were dying. Even the conservative Hopi communities were accepting change by the mid-1950s. Polingaysi Qoyawayma, Hopi potter and teacher, noted in her autobiography: "Half a century ago, Hopi people opposed education violently; now they became aware of its many advantages. Where they had once accepted it rebelliously, they now sought it for their children."[20]

In 1961, a nationwide Indian conference was held at the University of Chicago at which approximately five hundred Indians representing seventy different tribes participated. D'Arcy McNickle (Métis), a member of the Flathead reservation in Montana who had long been absent from his homeland, was the major conference organizer. The outcome of the gathering was "A Declaration of Indian Purpose," drafted by the participants, which temporarily unified them as Indian nations and challenged the termination of Indian tribes by the federal government.

McNickle was among the earliest Native people to publish a novel, *The Surrounded* (1936), and his career included working for John Collier, the commissioner of Indian Affairs during the 1930s and 1940s. Among his major activities was to bring Indians together to discuss their concerns. One of his last organizational efforts was the American Indian Chicago conference, about which he recalled:

> Reservation Indians were especially distrustful of their urbanized kinsmen, whom they suspected of scheming to liquidate tribal resources and claim their share. The conference was significant not only because the tribal participants found it possible to work their way through divisive counter moves, but out of their deliberations emerged issues and personalities which in the next few years would greatly affect the forces operating in Indian affairs.[21]

The conference established the significant role Indian leaders had in seeking to be self-governing and in challenging the federal termination policies that were underway in Indian country.

▶ ———

Connecting My Story to the Larger Story

In 1961, my father was elected lieutenant governor of Santa Clara Pueblo. He was among the Pueblo Indian delegation that attended the American Indian Chicago conference. Inspired by the meeting, he and other council members began plans to improve our community. Funds became available to construct a tribal center and a rehabilitation facility to treat alcoholism, and to make improvements within Santa Clara Canyon for the purpose of building the pueblo's economy. It was a progressive period.

Federal Indian policies were personally important to me because they affected our daily lives. Conversations at the dinner table between my parents and relatives who stopped by to visit in the evenings often included discussions about the federal policy of termination. A sense of urgency prevailed about termination if it were ever enacted. It made my parents value education more, and they pressed me, the oldest of their five children, to do well in school.

I attended the Santa Clara Pueblo Day School at the reservation, located about twenty-five miles north of Santa Fe and ten miles as the crow flies east of Los Alamos, New Mexico. The school is operated by the Bureau of Indian Affairs and has a parent advisory board. Students moved into a new school building in 1997. Most Santa Clara Pueblo children complete their primary education at the day school and begin seventh grade at the public school in Espanola or, if accepted, the Santa Fe Indian School.

After completing third grade at the Santa Clara Day School, my parents enrolled me at the Espanola Elementary School, the local public school located in the small city of Espanola adjacent to the Pueblo. My parents were seeking a broader education for me in the hope I would one day attend and graduate from college. At first, attending the public school was distinctly different since my classmates were primarily Spanish and Anglo, and I was forced to make the transition each school day from the security of the Pueblo community to the unfamiliarity of my non-Pueblo classmates. I did, however, learn the art of survival within the public school system.

Pueblo life was never the same after the introduction of television. Instead of sitting around the dining table with coffee telling stories with relatives, the men watched wrestling on Friday night, and women talked about soap operas. My parents acquired a television set when I was about eleven years old. In time, I changed, too, becoming influenced by the television and desiring to see for myself cities and places around the world. I discovered a book at home by Theodora Kroeber about "Ishi." The cover photograph of Ishi triggered a connection for me with my own developing sense of being an "Indian." Attending the public school had made me aware that I was different, and although I did my best to hide being different by learning to ski and play in the school band, I was identified as a "squaw" in front of my classmates by a seventh-grade teacher. At the time, my image of a "squaw" was of a white woman in buckskin wearing a headband with a feather stuck in it, and clearly not me. During the summer of 1969, the seed of my interest in filmmaking was planted. I was fourteen years old when a Hollywood film crew came to Santa Clara Pueblo to make a movie starring Anthony Quinn, who portrayed a character named Flapping Eagle, a drunken Indian with a ludicrous plan to protest injustices committed against Indians by stealing a railroad car. The movie script for *Flap* (1970, Warner Brothers) was loosely based on a popular book by Clair Huffaker, a non-Indian, titled *Nobody Loves a Drunken Indian.*[22]

That the firsthand opportunity to watch the production of a movie, including the building of a facade, the application of makeup on actors, and hearing the director call out "action," took place about a five-minute walk from my house is still amazing to me. The Pueblo community was allowed to watch the action. I was starstruck, but not by the actors; rather, my soul desired to be a film director. Carol Reed, the director, sat in a director's chair with his name on it, on a crane above the set. He wore the classic beret and held a bullhorn that he used to shout his directives.

My fresh interest in filmmaking was overshadowed by a group of young Indians who appeared in local newscasts criticizing the filming of *Flap* and another major film, *A Man Called Horse,* which was filmed in the Northern Plains. These AIM members impressed me for being outspoken in front of television news cameras and for making news headlines openly criticizing the failure of government policies for Indians. Despite AIM protests, both movies were released in 1970, several months apart. *A Man Called Horse* (1970, National General) was a box office success; it was also replete with Plains Indian lore and Hollywood's claim of authenticating a Sioux "Sun vow." *Flap* was in theaters less than a month, with the main character's role of a drunk Indian rebel reduced to caricature. My community, Santa Clara Pueblo, was merely a backdrop for this awful movie about Indians.

In August 1971, I enrolled at the College of Santa Fe and was introduced to American Indians from different tribes who were participating in an independent filmmaking workshop in Santa Fe. Some members of the group were students at the Institute of American Indian Arts, located down the street from the college. The group left after my first semester. After graduating in 1975, I began graduate school. I often wondered what happened to that early group of film students. Eventually, in 1979, I began pursuing my interest in media. I wrote a proposal that was funded by the Youth Grants Office of the National Endowment for the Humanities to produce a video about the growing participation of Pueblo Indians in powwows that originated with Plains Indians. In 1980, I became a coproducer and host of a public affairs television program, *Pueblo Voices,* a bimonthly broadcast for the ABC-TV affiliate station in Albuquerque. After making several major changes in my personal life, in 1984 I enrolled in a documentary filmmaking program at the Anthropology Film Center in Santa Fe. After completing the one-year program, my life as a video maker began in earnest.

The last fifteen years have been important ones for Indians, including myself. Our efforts to participate in dialogues internationally and nationally in all fields of inquiry, including history, literature, and science are increasing, but continued efforts are necessary to correct the historically narrow view of "Indians" as limited in their capacity to participate at all, especially as filmmakers. Of the thousand or so professional films and videos made by Native Americans, only a select few have been seen on

Adrianna Ignacio (Wampanoag) in *Hózhó of Native Women* (1997), director Beverly R. Singer.

public television or cable TV because of limited distribution and narrowly defined programming interests. Native films and videos do not fit neatly into program categories of drama, sitcom, environmental, or nature programs because our films and videos integrate such themes and reflect our political identities. As such, our films are more challenging to program on public television and are not programmed by commercial television stations largely due to the political nature of our stories, which force viewers to listen and watch "Indians" who are thoughtful, educated, provocative, and funny. These images do not conform to the stereotypes that persist in films about Indians that have remained the norm.

[4] *Native Filmmakers, Programs, and Institutions*

▶

When We Took Up Cameras

Filmmaking is the white man's craft that betrayed Native Americans and promoted our demise. Filmmaking is a novel art for Native Americans, considering the antiquity of Aboriginal, American Indian, and Alaska Native art traditions that existed long before European contact. But during the last thirty years, Native Americans have been learning how to produce, direct, and write films and video programs, and we now have over a thousand titles to our credit. Native filmmakers have documented the social and cultural reaffirmation among indigenous people that has taken place since the mid-1960s. In this chapter I review the development of Native American filmmaking and survey films and videos that were produced, directed, or written by Native people.

▶

Programs and Institutions

In 1966, John Adair, an anthropologist working in collaboration with filmmaker Sol Worth, initiated the first filmmaking project in the United States with a group of Navajo at their reservation. Worth and Adair wrote a proposal to the National Science Foundation in cooperation with the Annenberg School of Communications at the University of Pennsylvania to study the effects of and approach to filmmaking among a culturally distinct people. Their plan was to teach very basic film skills without the cultural overlay of ideas about film aesthetics based on Western film practice, and then have their subjects depict their culture in their own way.[1] Their project took place at Pine Springs, Arizona. Seven Navajo young adults completed eight practice films and seven edited 16mm films. The "Navajo films," as they came to be called, are a unique body of work that reflect the combined goals of anthropology and a filmmaking study.

Adair and Worth's attempt to hand over the creative process to their project participants was nominally successful. The completed Navajo films document daily tasks and cultural art practices such as weaving and silversmithing. One of the films used a narrative by following a rolling wheel to a lake, creating mystery and a unique view of the surrounding area. The films were intended to serve as an anthropological case study and not as films to be publicly distributed. The project had a short lifespan and did not continue beyond its initial conception as a research study. Not even Margaret Mead, matriarch of anthropology, who supported the use of photography and filmmaking in the study of non-Western cultures, had let go of the camera.[2] There since has been no project similar in focus or intent as Adair and Worth's Navajo film study.[3]

In 1968, the American Film Institute (AFI) created the Community Film Workshop Council, which started filmmaking workshops in thirty-five communities with the intent to engage inner-city and rural youth in producing media in their communities.[4] Bruce Ignacio (Northern Ute), who participated in the Community Film Workshop in Santa Fe, says that he entered the program basically by accident:

Dean Bear Claw, director of *Warrior Chiefs in a New Age* (1991), with his son. Photograph courtesy of Native Voices Public TV, Bozeman, Montana.

I had gone to Santa Fe, and I was getting ready to go to Rhode Island School of Design in the fall of 1971. I was working for plant management at the Institute of American Indian Arts, and the Community Film Workshop had just started. George Burdeau and Ollie Miller, a black guy, talked me into joining the group. That's how I became involved with the Film Workshop. . . . Basically the workshop trained Puerto Rican and Black young filmmakers. At that time it was very hard for minorities to get into filmmaking at any level.[5]

Among the participants Ignacio remembers in the workshop were Don Whitesinger, Milo Yellow Hair, Tommy Montoya, Richard Whitman, Stan Zuni, Bill Soza, and Tommy Fields. They were taught technical aspects of running a camera, working with the audio recorders, and other basic technical aspects of filmmaking.[6] Apprenticeship programs were developed for some of the workshop participants, including positions at television stations in Albuquerque, Chicago, and Los Angeles. Ignacio recalls that the participants talked about filmmaking in the same way that Native people do now, but at that time he found it especially hard and expensive to pursue filmmaking.

The Anthropology Film Center was founded in Santa Fe by filmmakers Carroll and Joan Willliams, who had worked closely with the Santa Fe Community Film Workshop. The Anthropology Film Center provided "macro-intensive training in the technical and theoretical bases of 16mm film production."[7] Several Native Americans, including George Burdeau, Larry Littlebird, Larry Cesspooch, Gloria Bird, Joy Harjo, Ava Hamilton, Rain Parrish, Marcus Amerman, and myself, received film training at the Center.

It wasn't until the seventies that the Federal Communications Commission (FCC) issued a mandate requiring local television stations to offer broadcast time to underserved populations such as Native American tribes. In order to receive an FCC broadcast license, television stations complied with the order, creating the first opportunity for Native Americans to begin producing their own public affairs television programs in the United States. *Indian Country Today* was one of the first programs to result from the mandate when the station manager of KFYR-TV, an NBC-affiliate station in Bismarck, North Dakota, approached the Standing Rock Sioux Tribe about cooperating on a program. The program began broadcasting in October 1973 and featured interviews with community leaders, educators, and spokespeople concerned with social, economic, political, and health issues affecting Indians in South Dakota.

The show was hosted, directed, and produced by Harriet Skye, a member of the Standing Rock Sioux Tribe. Skye's involvement as a Native American in television broadcasting was unheard of in the early seventies.

She recalls that the show brought "Indian people into [the] living rooms [of white people who otherwise] wouldn't allow an Indian inside their house."[8] Although the Standing Rock Sioux Tribe later released sponsorship of the program (it was picked up by the United Tribes Technical and Educational College and later turned over to the American Indian Historical Society in San Francisco), Skye remained the producer and host throughout the long run of the program, which ran its final episode in December 1984. The significance and participation of Native Americans in media at the regional level was an important opportunity to bridge the social distance that existed between Indian communities and non-Indians. Programs similar to *Indian Country Today* were hosted by Chester Yazzie in Flagstaff; John Belindo in Albuquerque; Ray Murdock in Bemidji, Minnesota; Sammy Tonekei White in Oklahoma City; and Tim Giago in Rapid City, South Dakota.

In 1972, KYUK-TV in Bethel, Alaska, began collaboration with Yupik communities in Southwest Alaska in the production of news broadcasts in the Yupik and Inupiat languages. Alexie Isaac (Yupik) was hired by KYUK-TV as a producer and director at the station. Isaac directed numerous award-winning productions, including *Yupiit Yuraryarait/A Dancing People* (1983) and *Eyes of the Spirit* (1984), which he coproduced with writer Corey Flintoff, a National Public Radio host. The stories are celebrations of Alaska Natives' revival of mask carving and mask dancing.

In 1974 NBC-TV in Los Angeles initiated and sponsored *The Native American Series* and was eventually pressured to hire Sandra Osawa (Makah) to coproduce, direct, and write the scripts. The series presented a contemporary mirror of Native stories, historical reviews, artistic expression, and a new view of Indian identity that was not based on old photographs of dead Indians. Instead, acting performances and musical performers, such as Buffy Sainte-Marie, were presented alongside interviews with non-Indians concerned with Native political issues. Osawa recalled the process whereby she came to be involved with the series:

> I was working at the Los Angeles Indian Center editing the *Talking Leaf.* There was conflict over what we wanted to do with the paper; some staff wanted an important news magazine journal tailored to investigating native issues. To put it in the context of the times, I remember Russell Means was giving press conferences in L.A., running from the F.B.I., and there was a lot of media hype and attention involving A.I.M. A few people in the community went to NBC and said, "Hey, we'd like to see something on Indians. . . . . You haven't shown anything." Stella Montoya and her husband were among the key figures. They held a series of meetings with NBC, who already gave public affairs money to the Asian Americans, Chicanos, Blacks. They hadn't given any to Native Americans. NBC indicated a possible project but asked: "Who do you have?" Stella mentioned "Sandy's really interested in media." I think it

Sandra Osawa with Marlon Brando, *The Native American Series*, NBC-TV, 1975.
Photograph courtesy of Upstream Productions.

was because of my writing. I met with NBC and they asked, "Could you outline ten programs?" I completed the outline and took a conservative approach.
NBC liked the ten topic ideas I proposed. They said, "Well, you don't have any
experience so maybe we could pair you with someone who's had experience.
Then Montoya informed NBC: "No, we don't want it the same old way. . . .
we want it Indian produced, Indian written."[9]

Osawa also recalls that she and other Native Americans protested about another Indian project NBC was sponsoring called "Circle Your Wagons" because it was being produced by a white man:

> Stella was really effective organizing and getting letters of support for our project. A friend of ours in Washington State representing the American Indian Movement called NBC, and the production shut down. The thing going on was that the Emmy-winning producer didn't want any Indians on his staff. We started making noise and he agreed, "O.K. I'll have an associate producer be an Indian." He didn't get his token Indian. Had he gotten a token Indian to come along and rubber-stamp the idea he probably would have been successful in doing his series. It was just beautiful the way it worked out. Our series happened like we dreamed it would. I think it's the first time in the country that there was an Indian television series produced, written, and featuring Native American performers including Charlie Hill, Floyd Westerman, Buffy Sainte-Marie, and Frank Salcedo, who later portrayed Chief Joseph for a public television production. (Marlon Brando also made an appearance in support of the project.)[10]

The Native American Series was nationally broadcast in 1975 by stations in New York, Dallas, Los Angeles, and Chicago. In spite of being aired at 6:30 A.M., just prior to the *Today Show,* the show found an audience, including teachers who wrote to her asking that the program be broadcast at a "decent hour." Osawa received an outstanding producer award from NBC for the production of *The Native American Series.*

In 1975, the Emergency School Aid Act (ESAA) was implemented by the U.S. Office of Education with the specific purpose of creating an educational television series consisting of documentaries about Indian tribes. The Office of Education provided a production grant to the Northeast Wisconsin In-School Tele-Communications Program to cooperate with the University of Wisconsin at Green Bay and produce the *Forest Spirits Series.* George Burdeau (Blackfeet) served as project coordinator for the production titled *Living with Tradition.* The program was one of the first major film projects to be organized by a Native American. The film is about the impact of federal termination on the Menominee Tribe in Wisconsin and their struggle to retain their tribal status in order to preserve their cultural traditions and shared ownership of their homelands. The *Forest Spirit Series* consisted of seven programs about the Oneida and Menominee Tribes; of these, *Living with Tradition* was the only one with a Native filmmaker in a key production role.

In the early seventies, Richard Whitman (Yuchi/Creek) was a student at the Institute of American Indian Arts where he worked on a film about the school titled *Red Reflections of Life: The Institute of American Indian*

Arts (1973). The film featured Whitman and another student from Zuni who both discuss significant influences in their lives as developing artists. As an actor, Whitman portrayed Carter Camp, an Indian activist in *Lakota Woman* (1994), a film produced for Turner Network Television (TNT). Today, Whitman is an established artist and photographer.

In 1976, numerous projects involving American Indians were developed in anticipation of the U.S. bicentennial celebration. A series of projects were sponsored by the Bureau of Indian Affairs titled *The Native American: A Cultural Projection*. They included an exhibition of contemporary American Indian art, literature and oratory events, and a video documentary component. The video project was intended to "produce and edit documentary programs of tribal activities as designated by individual tribes." The objective of the video project was "to train Native Americans to do both the basic videotaping and editing."[11] Twenty Native Americans from different communities traveled to Washington, D.C., for a week of basic hands-on training in the operation of portable videotape and editing equipment. They worked in teams and were sent out to document a variety of tribally selected activities and people. The teams returned to Washington, D.C., where they were assisted in editing the programs by a private production company contracted by the BIA. In all, forty-four programs were produced, and each participating tribe received a copy of their program. The edited master videotapes were cataloged and indexed as the "Native American Videotape Archives," and given to the Institute of American Indian Arts Museum collection in Santa Fe, New Mexico.

In 1977, the Native American Public Broadcasting Consortium (NAPBC) was founded and sponsored by the Corporation for Public Broadcasting (CPB) and the Public Broadcasting Service (PBS) as a nonprofit media organization in Lincoln, Nebraska. Frank Blythe (Sioux/Eastern Cherokee) has served as executive director since its inception. The media scope and services of the Native American organization was similar to the Black, Latino, and Asian consortia organized with support from the CPB. The consortia were concerned with producing programs for public television reflecting the populations they represented. Between 1977 and 1980, the Native American Public Broadcasting Consortium held annual meetings concerned with development of media including TV and film projects in several major cities including Los Angeles. NAPBC used this period to cultivate interest among Native American tribes to participate in developing their own media, which led to the initiation of several tribal media projects. In 1986 NAPBC produced *American Indian Artists,* a three-part series that featured the art and lives of Dan Namingha (Hopi/Tewa), Jaune Quick-To-See Smith (Shoshone/French/Cree), and Larry Golsh (Pala Mission Indian).[12]

The Native American Public Broadcasting Consortium was renamed Native American Public Telecommunications, Inc. (NAPT) in 1995. With a board of directors comprised of Native and non-Native members, its current mission is "to produce and encourage the production and successful use of quality public telecommunications programs by and about Native Americans for both Native American and general audiences."[13] Grants administration is a major function of the organization, with the major portion of funds given to public television programs that are able to compete for national and local broadcast time. White filmmakers have received grants directly from NAPT to work collaboratively with Native producers, which has raised concern among Native filmmakers, myself included, who think the grants should be made to Native Americans who then can hire whites to work with us. The primary criteria for the funding of projects is based on their viability for being shown on public television. There are no particular restrictions as to who can receive money for projects as long as Native Americans have key roles, such as directing or producing the production. Nonetheless, NAPT has an impressive list of productions, including a recent celebrated series titled *Storytellers of the Pacific* (1996), which is told by Native people in their communities along the Pacific Rim.

The Real People was an ambitious eight-part series developed in 1976 by KSPS-TV, a public television station in Spokane, Washington. It was developed prior to the establishment of the NAPBC. The series focused attention on lesser-known Indians located in the Northwest Plateau region of the United States. Among the tribes featured in the series were the Coeur d'Alene, Colville, Flathead, Kalispel, Kootenai, Nez Perce, and Spokane. George Burdeau was a consultant for *The Real People* series.

People of the First Light was produced by WGBY-TV in Springfield, Massachusetts, in 1979. It consisted of seven programs that focused on New England and included Indians in Boston, the Wampanoag at Gay Head, the Mashpee at Cape Cod, the Narragansett in Rhode Island, and the Passamaquoddy in Maine.[14] Russell Peters (Mashpee/Wampanoag), who was active in Indian affairs throughout his life, was a coproducer and writer for the series. *People of the First Light* was significant for two reasons: first, from the perspective of having the direct participation of tribal representatives such as Peters, and second, because it was the first public television series to call attention to Indians in the Northeast, who were the first to have contact with the Pilgrims and yet the last to be recognized as part of the American story.

Also in 1979, the Alaska Department of Education funded the University of Alaska at Fairbanks to collaborate with Northwest Arctic Television in Kotzebue to create a series of documentary programs about Inuit culture.

The Alaska Native Heritage Film Project produced a series of films that involved some production training of Alaska Natives.

The Ute Tribal Media Department was established in 1979 at Fort Duchesne, Utah. Larry Cesspooch, the director of the department, produced over a hundred videotapes that documented tribal history and narrative stories retold by elder members of the Uintah and Ouray Ute tribe. Cesspooch actively sought community involvement, as artist Dan Lomahaftewa (Hopi/Choctaw), a resident at the Ute reservation at the time, recalls: "Larry asked me to help him with one of his video projects, and I agreed. . . . we had a good time acting like ourselves for the camera."[15]

In 1980 the U.S. Office of Education began sponsoring the Ethnic Heritage Program to provide tribal governments with media grants. The grants were intended to support videotape projects concerned with cultural preservation and the collection of interviews with community elders, many of whom retold tribal stories.

The Mississippi Band of Choctaw Indians and the Creek Nation of Oklahoma received grants from the Ethnic Heritage Program in 1982. Filmmaker Gary Robinson (Choctaw/Cherokee) was hired by the Creek Nation and recounts his experience:

> We started a series of educational programs with people in the community who came to me and said, "There's a need for this kind of program out there" or "We need a program about this contemporary issue that affects the tribe." I had people coming from the community, like Indian educators, Indian community leaders saying, "There's nothing out there for our children in the schools about our own people." We would talk about what would be useful, and I always took my leads from them. We did a program on the Green Corn ceremony, the main annual traditional ceremony of the tribe. A lot of the people in the community were church members and had distanced themselves from the traditional community. Friction between the traditional ceremonial practitioners and the Christian community is very strong. I used their differing positions within the community to foster a better understanding. We produced the program and broadcast it locally; both the Creek community and the larger community soaked up the program like a sponge.[16]

Between 1980 and 1990, print journalism for U.S. Native communities was easier and less costly to establish than were media production centers. Thus, the greater emphasis in media was on the production of tribe-based newspapers. In 1982, Tim Giago (Lakota) founded the *Lakota Times*, now called *Indian Country Today*, an internationally distributed newspaper featuring national Indian news features.

The greater significance of this ten-year period for Native film and video production is that it represents the first attempts by individual Native

Americans to produce and direct their own films and videos; among the original independent directors were Victor Masayesva Jr. (Hopi), Phil Lucas (Choctaw), and Sandra Osawa (Makah).

In 1990, Native Voices Public Television Workshop was established by Daniel Hart, professor of film at Montana State University in Bozeman, in order to support independent productions by Native Americans for public television. Basic financial support is given to producers based on proposal submissions, and producers are given access to KUSM-TV facilities and assisted by personnel at the station.[17] In 1991 Dean Bear Claw (Crow) was accepted at Native Voices Television Workshop based on a script he submitted. Bear Claw directed *Warrior Chiefs in a New Age,* an award-winning program about Plenty Coups and Medicine Crow, Crow leaders who envisaged the future of their people and the arrival of whites to their territory. Bear Claw continued his education at New York University and in 1997 began postgraduate study at the University of California, Berkeley.

Native Voices produced several major historical programs including *The Place of the Falling Waters* (1991), produced by Roy Bigcrane (Flathead) in collaboration with historian Thompson Smith. It is a three-part program about the Flathead Indian Reservation and the impact of a hydroelectric dam built on the reservation. Bigcrane continues his media production as an employee of the Salish Kootenai Community College at the Flathead Reservation in Montana.

Transitions: The Death of the Mother Tongue (1991), by Darrell Robes Kipp and Joe Fisher, is a Native Voices Public Television Workshop production by two Blackfeet filmmakers who draw attention to cultural loss in their examination of the demise of the Blackfeet language, a mother tongue that is no longer the primary language spoken at the reservation as a result of forced assimilation. Kipp remains actively involved in Blackfeet language preservation, and both he and Fisher continue to work on film projects in Montana.

Three additional programs by the Native Voices Workshop involve the work of artists. The first is *The Crow Mapuche Connection* by Susan Stewart (Crow), who collaborated with a Soviet director named Arvo Iho to examine a connection between art made by indigenous people in North and South America. A second program about a Blackfeet artist was directed by Terry Macy (Warm Springs). *Ernie Peppion: The Art of Healing* is a portrait of an artist who was in a car collision that left him quadriplegic and the remarkable paintings he produces invoking his physical disability.

Among current support for indigenous filmmakers is the Center for Media, Culture, and History, established at New York University and di-

Still from *Transitions: The Death of the Mother Tongue* (1991) by Darrell Robes Kipp and Joe Fisher.

rected by anthropology professor and media scholar Faye Ginsburg. The Center at NYU sponsored several Native American filmmakers with Rockefeller Humanities Fellowships and United Nations Environmental Programme Media Fellowship residencies. Recipients of the fellowships were Dean Bear Claw, Sandra Osawa, Harriet Skye, and Loretta Todd. The Rockefeller Foundation also sponsors an Intercultural Media Fellowship, whose support of Native filmmakers has included Ava Hamilton, Arlene Bowman, George Burdeau, Chris Eyre, Victor Masayesva Jr., Randy Redroad, and Loretta Todd.

The Film and Video Center of the Smithsonian National Museum of the American Indian is among the major centers for data collection and information about Native American film and video production, radio, and new media produced by indigenous people from the Americas. Located in New York City, the Film and Video Center began as the Native American Film and Video Project at the Museum of the American Indian and was organized by Elizabeth Weatherford in the 1970s, who continues in her role as head of the center today. In 1979, the first Native American Film and Video Festival was held in New York, during which more than 125 films and videos about Native Americans were presented over a three-month period. On November 28, 1989, stewardship of the Heye Foundation Museum of the American Indian was transferred to the Smithsonian Institution along with a commitment to indigenous leadership and staffing. The Film and Video Center has grown into an international center dedicated to the promotion of indigenous American media.

The Native American Film and Video Festival is the largest biennnial gathering of its kind in the United States, and has presented more than four hundred films and videos, the majority of which have been Native productions from North, Central, and South America made in the last ten years. In addition to screening films and videos, panel discussions about Native media and special programming efforts by Native communities, such as the Inuit Broadcasting Corporation in Nunavit (the Inuit territory in Canada), the Ute Indian Tribe in the United States, and the Video in the Villages Project in Brazil, highlight the festival programming. The center also assists researchers and filmmakers with related media information, sponsors special programs such as the summer series "Thursday Night at the Movies," and presents other public programs by visiting film and video makers at the Museum.

Filmmakers

There is no doubt that the funding and institutional support described above made it possible for Native Americans to start taking control of their own images, but without the creativity and persistence of dozens of Native Americans who wrote, produced, and directed the films and videos, there would be no book for me to write. In the remainder of this chapter, I will focus on some of the key individuals involved in the development of Native American media.

Bob Hicks

Bob Hicks (Creek/Seminole) was the first Native American to graduate from the Director's Program of the American Film Institute. In 1979, he began writing a short thesis film titled *Return of the Country,* which he produced in 1982. Writer and legal scholar Rennard Strickland (Cherokee) describes Hicks's film: "A brilliant ironic perspective dominates the sequences, done as if in a dream [the structure of the film *is* a dream]. *Return of the Country* turns the tables, with an Indian President and the formation of a Bureau of Caucasian Affairs, which is instructed to enforce policies to help acculturate little Anglo boys and girls into the new mainstream Indian culture."[18]

Prior to attending the American Film Institute, Hicks worked in

Oklahoma as a theater stage manager and director between 1974 and 1976. His desire to learn filmmaking led him to apply to the American Film Institute after attending a talk by an AFI representative:

> I read in the local newspaper that this lady from the American Film Institute was coming to give a talk. I went down there that night and heard her talk. She showed some films made by their students. They was great. I couldn't believe it. I met her afterwards and she gave me one of her brochures, and I looked at the board of directors. It was like the who's who of Hollywood. I took the top three names, wrote them a letter and said I'm interested in going to film school and needed advice. Two of them answered me back; Charlton Heston wrote me a real nice letter encouraging me, plus he sent me a catalog from AFI. I was reading it and they had the kind of curriculum that I really wanted. I was getting all my catalogs from NYU and USC, and I would have to start as a freshman and wait until I'm a junior to really go into filmmaking. I said, "I can't wait that long." I sent my application to AFI, and the deadline was January, and they don't let you know till June. I get my answer back, and I'm accepted, and the school starts in September. This is June, and I don't have any money. I sell my car shop, restoring antique cars. At one time I was making great bucks, but the economy had shifted, plus my heart was no longer in it either. I got a buyer and paid off my small business loan. I went out to raise money to come to Los Angeles. In September of 1979, I headed for Hollywood. I felt like the *Grapes of Wrath*. . . . I loaded up my car and I was leaving Oklahoma. I arrived here, Los Angeles, and went to the AFI, and it was tucked away in the Hollywood Hills. AFI was in this huge mansion, and I arrived there with 70 other students. I didn't realize they get like 700 applications and only accept 75. I went there that year and I was so thankful that I got to do it. It is the kind of curriculum where they look at your work after your first year, and if they think you have the talent, you're invited back to make a film. I was invited back. When I first got accepted at AFI, that theater company I was associated with in Tulsa had a benefit concert for me and helped to send me out.[19]

Hicks remained in Los Angeles and serves as chairman of the First Americans in the Arts, an organization that sponsors an awards ceremony acknowledging Native and non-Native professionals in the entertainment industry.

■───

Sandra Osawa

After her successful role producing and directing *The Native American Series* for television in Los Angeles, Sandra Osawa became an independent filmmaker and went on to establish Upstream Productions in Seattle with her husband, Yasu Osawa. In 1988, their first production, *In the Heart of Big Mountain,* was broadcast on the Learning Channel. The film is about the Hopi and Navajo (Dine) boundary dispute and the pending displacement of three hundred Navajo families residing at Big Mountain, Arizona. Osawa focused on one family with a larger struggle to protect themselves from exploitation by Peabody Coal Company, which is interested in coal deposits near Big Mountain. Osawa's productions represent a strong political and historical perspective with regard to Native American rights and self-determination.

In 1995, the highly competitive public television documentary series P.O.V. selected Osawa's *Lighting the 7th Fire,* a documentary about the Chippewa fishing rights controversy in Wisconsin, to be broadcast at prime time on July 4, 1996.[20] Another documentary, *Pepper's Powwow* (1995), was nationally broadcast by public television stations in July 1997. The film is about Jim Pepper, a jazz saxophonist of Creek/Kaw ancestry who integrated jazz and Native musical compositions. In 1998, Osawa completed *Usual and Accustomed Places,* another major documentary, about the Makah and other tribes in the Northwest whose history is reviewed in an examination of their fishing and hunting treaties. She recently completed a biography about the life of Oneida comedian Charlie Hill titled *On and Off the Res with Charlie Hill* (2000).

■————————————————————————————————————

Phil Lucas

Phil Lucas (Choctaw) graduated with a degree in science and visual communication from Western Washington University in Bellingham in 1970. His first film project, *Images of Indians,* was produced between 1979 and 1981 as a five-part series for public television. It critically examines Hollywood movies and Indian stereotypes. Lucas served as writer and as coproducer and codirector with Robert Hagopian.[21] Each segment examines different Hollywood movies that illustrate and explain how Indians are misrepresented culturally and historically.

Lucas established Phil Lucas Productions in 1980 in Issaquah, Washington. In 1986, he produced *The Honour of All,* a groundbreaking film that reenacted the story of an Aboriginal community named Alkali Lake in Canada that successfully reversed the problem of alcoholism through realignment with indigenous spiritual beliefs and practices. In 1993, Lucas served as coproducer of *The Broken Chain,* a televised drama produced by Turner Broadcasting about the Iroquois Confederacy that was broadcast on Turner Network Television (TNT). Also in 1993, Lucas codirected *Dances for the New Generation* with Hanay Geiogamah (Kiowa), a documentary about the American Indian Dance Theater for public television

On the banks of the Nisqually River, near Olympia, Washington, Billy Frank Jr. talks about his childhood in *Storytellers of the Pacific* (1996). Left to right: Gary Robinson, director of photography; Phil Lucas, producer/director; Amy Echohawk, production assistant trainee; Tom Williams, second camera; Jan Cyr, sound recordist; and Billy Frank Jr. Photograph courtesy of Native American Public Telecommunications.

based on the dance company's 1989 performance of dances representing different tribes for "Great Performances, Dance in America Series." The film was broadcast on public television in 1994.

Chris Spotted Eagle

Another filmmaker, Chris Spotted Eagle (Houma), formed a production company in Minneapolis. He produced several films in the 1980s. *The Great Spirit within the Hole* (1983) was meant to raise awareness about the violation of Native American religious freedom in federal prisons. *Our Sacred Land* (1984) is about the spiritual and historical significance of the Black Hills to the Sioux Nation and their struggle to reclaim it.

George Horse Capture, Larry Littlebird, and Larry Cesspooch

I'd Rather Be Powwowing was produced for public television in 1983 by a Native American production team funded by the Corporation for Public

Broadcasting. The production included George Horse Capture (Gros Ventre), producer; Larry Littlebird (Laguna/Santo Domingo), director; and Larry Cesspooch (Northern Ute), sound mixer. The film was about a Native family man who travels to participate in powwows during the summer months.

■───

Arlene Bowman

Arlene Bowman (Navajo) is a graduate of the University of California at Los Angeles, Motion Picture Television Department. Her thesis film, *Navajo Talking Picture* (1986), is about her return to the Navajo Reservation to reacquaint herself with her grandmother by making a film about her. Despite her grandmother's refusal to be the subject of her film, Bowman persisted, setting the stage for a serious conflict between herself and her grandmother. The film raised important questions about the approach used by Bowman to make her film and highlights broken ties with one's community. *Navajo Talking Picture* is critically examined in chapter 5. In 1993, Bowman received grants from the Rockefeller Foundation Media Program and the Independent Television Service (ITVS) to coproduce and direct *The Song Journey: Traditional Native Women Singers* (1994) with Jeanne Moret, and produced a short dance video titled *Men and Women Are Good Dancers* (1994).

■───

Milo Yellowhair

In 1990, Milo Yellowhair (Lakota) cowrote and narrated *In the Spirit of Crazy Horse,* a program for the national public television news series *Frontline.* Yellowhair's narration gave personal context to the history of the Great Sioux Nation and the dispossession of the Black Hills in South Dakota. Yellowhair is from the Pine Ridge Reservation and attended the Institute of American Indian Arts in the early 1970s, but as tensions mounted at his reservation in 1973, he returned home. *In the Spirit of Crazy Horse* reviews the history since the original Wounded Knee Massacre in 1890 carried out by the U.S. Calvary, and examines the events leading to a military standoff between the FBI and the American Indian Movement at Wounded Knee in 1973. Yellowhair remains active in seeking the return of the Black Hills to his people.

Diane Reyna

Diane Reyna (Taos/San Juan Pueblo) directed *Surviving Columbus: The Story of the Pueblo People* (1992), a retelling of Pueblo cultural history that charts their response to the arrival of Spanish conquistadors to their territory, the Pueblo Revolt against Spanish colonization in 1680, and the Mexican occupation of the geographic Southwest and concludes with the American present. The Peabody Award–winning program was broadcast nationally on public television, and was coproduced with KNME-TV in Albuquerque and Native Images, a former production unit of the Communication Arts Program at the Institute of American Indian Arts in Santa Fe.

Surviving Columbus was Diane Reyna's directoral debut after working for eighteen years as a news camera operator for KOAT-TV, the ABC affiliate in Albuquerque. Prior to starting the project, Reyna was teaching at the Institute of American Indian Arts. George Burdeau was the executive producer for *Surviving Columbus,* and Nedra Darling (Potawatomi) was coproducer for the program. Conroy Chino and Simon Ortiz, both from Acoma Pueblo, participated as narrator and writer for the program, lending a personal context to the events leading up to the 1680 Pueblo revolt in which Acoma played a key role.

George Burdeau

The first Native American to be a member of the Directors Guild of America was George Burdeau (Blackfeet). He was among the first group of students to attend the Institute of American Indian Arts in 1962. In the 1970s he moved to Los Angeles to pursue a filmmaking career and became etablished as a director. In 1989, he began a Communication Arts Program at the Institute of American Indian Arts. In his role as director, he reflected that Native Americans "have not had access to the medium for our own use, as well as for communicating with the rest of the world."[22] His most recent film, *Backbone of the World: The Blackfeet* (1997), is a personal story about his role as a filmmaker and the importance of being a member of the Blackfeet Nation. In 1997, at the premiere screening of the film at the Native American Film and Video Festival sponsored by the Smithsonian National Museum of the American Indian in New York City, Burdeau said this project was the highlight of his career because it took him home. *Backbone of the World: The Blackfeet* was produced by Pamela Roberts of Rattlesnake Productions; the line producer was Darren Robes Kipp (Blackfeet). The film was screened at the Sundance Film Festival in 1998.

Conroy Chino

Conroy Chino has been a career television news reporter in Albuquerque. He had a part in *Contact* (1997), a movie based on a screenplay by Carl Sagan. The movie featured Jodie Foster in the role of an astronomer who makes contact with extraterrestrial life. Chino said he was selected to portray a news reporter at a mob scene in the movie after the producers watched sample reels of several local reporters.[23] His career as a television news reporter came out of his being Native and from being

> influenced in the 60s and 70s by the Chicano and Black Civil Rights movements while in college. I considered myself an activist. I started working as an announcer for the *Singing Wire* radio program at KUNM-FM. One day, I scheduled a meeting with television news anchor Dick Knipfing at KOAT-TV in Albuquerque and told him of my interest in working there. He hired me and I began working as a photographer-reporter. At that time, they were still using film. My first experience began with up-to-the minute reports throughout the city, and later I moved into investigative reporting.[24]

Hattie Kaufman

Prior to becoming a national television correspondent and host for *CBS This Morning,* Hattie Kaufman (Nez Perce) was a television reporter for KING-TV in Seattle, beginning in 1981, and she became a news anchor there. In April 1987, Kaufman decided to "cast the line out into the big sea and see if anybody would bite."[25] ABC hired her as a correspondent for *Good Morning America.* After receiving an Emmy Award for her reports, she was hired as a correspondent and substitute morning host for *CBS This Morning.*

Ava Hamilton

The messages in stories that document issues affecting Native people today are also carried forward to the next generation through films such as *Everything Has a Spirit* (1992), codirected by Ava Hamilton (Arapaho/Cheyenne) and Gabriel Dech. This film details the federal government's role in deter-

Lakota spiritual leader Arvol Looking Horse in *Everything Has a Spirit* (1992), coproducer and director Ava Hamilton; Pat Howard, photographer. Photograph courtesy of Front Range Educational Media Corp. (KBDI-TV).

mining and limiting the religious freedom of American Indians. *Everything Has a Spirit* was written by novelist and poet Linda Hogan (Chickasaw) and attempts to balance the integrity of Native American ceremonial life and spirituality with the white laws that limit it. Ava Hamilton is a founding board member and coordinator of the Native American Producers Alliance.

Ruby Sooktis

NAPA member Ruby Sooktis (Cheyenne) pursued her goal to produce films about Cheyenne history. In 1992, she produced and directed *Season of Children,* a film addressing the problem of child abuse among the Northern Cheyenne. The film touched off a politically charged debate in the community that prevented it from being screened elsewhere. In 1995, she produced *Trek North 95,* a story about the Cheyenne's relocation in Oklahoma and their return to Montana in the nineteenth century. Sootkis believes that films that are being produced by independent Native American filmmakers represent a challenge to the status quo:

Native Americans' real history is so recent in filmmaking. We are caught in what has been defined, how we're supposed to behave, how we're supposed to be portrayed, and how we're supposed to react in different situations. I see the progress, but we still have to do more, not only in filmmaking, but also in our writing. The reason for that is that Native American writing from experiences, from living the culture, is from living their language. That's a big difference and every perspective is not recyclable. It's original. Original thinking, that's what's new about our participating as filmmakers. I think we need to be committed to all children's spiritual well-being with our own unique skills. I would like to think that when they're watching a movie a hundred years from now, or reading a book a hundred years from now, that it's not coming from a stranger.[26]

Harriet Skye

A film that will be remembered many years from now is Harriet Skye's *A Right to Be: The Story of an Indian Woman Who Took Back Control of Her Life* (1993), which she codirected and produced with Stefano Saraceni, an Italian director. The film documents her life story, which runs parallel with major changes in her community. Skye returns to her reservation after graduating with honors from New York University at the age of sixty-one. She revisits her alcoholism and the circumstances that led to her recovery from the disease. She draws parallels in her story with the ecological and emotional damage rendered by the Oahe Dam built on the Missouri River in the 1960s that flooded a major portion of farmland belonging to the Cheyenne River Sioux Reservation. The dam was constructed by the Army Corps of Engineers supposedly for flood control.

Mona Smith

Mona Smith (Dakota) is a filmmaker based in Minneapolis whose productions stress the need for the prevention of HIV/AIDS among Native Americans. *Her Giveaway: A Spiritual Journey with AIDS* (1988) features a Chippewa woman named Carol LaFavor who has AIDS and has refocused her life and illness to advocate for new approaches to prevention and treatment of HIV/AIDS. Two other programs by Smith are *Honored by the Moon* (1990) and *That Which Is Between* (1991), both of which present HIV/AIDS from a Native point of view that incorporates a healing narrative associated with nature.

Allen Jamieson

Independent productions from the Six Nations, representing Cayuga, Mohawk, Oneida, Onondaga, Seneca, and Tuscarora, are by filmmakers Allen Jamieson (Cayuga) and Melanie Printup Hope (Tuscarora). Jamieson is director of a nonprofit culture and media organization, Neto Hatinakwe Onkwehowe, in Buffalo, New York. He is the producer of *Indigenous Voices* (1992) and *Do:ge Gagwego o'jagwada't: We Stood Together* (1993), two videos that document the Native response to the imposition of a state tax on reservations in upstate New York.

Melanie Printup Hope

Melanie Printup Hope (Tuscarora) is a graduate of the Rensselaer Polytechnic Institute in Troy, New York. In addition to teaching college full-time, she is a multimedia artist whose installations combine new media technology with traditional art forms. Her early production *I Turn My Head* (1993) establishes a cultural polemic about her Native and white Euro-American heritage. *They've Seen the Land the Way It Was* (1993) is a video installation about cultural genocide of Cree and Inuit communities by the construction of a hydroelectric dam at James Bay in Northern Quebec. Hydro-Quebec is a public utility company owned by the Canadian government that has begun an enormous diversion of several rivers surrounding James Bay that will radically alter, and thereby destroy, the ecology of the region.[27] *The Prayer of Thanksgiving* is an interactive CD-ROM that combines the Haudenosaune Prayer of Thanksgiving for the Creation with beautiful graphic images of animals, plants, and other life forms and traditional music accompanying a recitation of the prayer. The installation was presented at the 1997 Smithsonian National Museum of the American Indian Film and Video Festival in New York City.

Randy Redroad

Younger Native Americans know that New York City is an artistic and literary center for independent creative endeavor. Randy Redroad (Cherokee) is a filmmaker who moved to New York City in the late eighties to pursue his goal of making films. He received film training at a workshop sponsored by Third World Newsreel in the city, an organization that has sponsored filmmaking workshops for about twenty years. It is a unique program that supports emerging filmmakers representing people of color.[28] Redroad completed two projects as the result of his participation in the workshop, *Cow Tipping: The Militant Indian Waiter* (1991) and *Haircuts Hurt* (1992). In 1994, he received a Rockefeller Intercultural Media grant and a script-writing residency at the Sundance Film Institute. *High Horse* (1994), a fiction narrative filmed entirely in New York City, is discussed in chapter 5. Redroad recently completed his first independent feature film, *Doe Boy* (2001), which was shown at the Sundance Festival.

Malinda Maynor

Filmmaker Malinda Maynor (Lumbee) graduated with a B.A. in history from Harvard University and left the East Coast to enroll in a graduate filmmaking program at Stanford University in 1995. While at Stanford, she completed two films, *Real Indians* (1996) and *Sounds of Faith* (1997). Both of her films counter the myths regarding Lumbee Indians in North Carolina and promote the view that the Native American experience is not limited to geography or physical appearance. She recently coproduced *In Light of Reverence* (2001) with filmmaker Terry McLeod.

Derron Twohatchet

Derron Twohatchet (Arapaho) received an arts fellowship residency at the Whitney Museum in New York City in 1995. His film *Detour* (1993) is an exploration of Native American homosexuality that is set apart by its use of 1940s film noir outtakes to exemplify the thoughts of a gay Native American character. Twohatchet's film is a dialectic work about homosexuality by a Native American.

Chris Eyre

Filmmaker Chris Eyre (Cheyenne/Arapaho) graduated from the prestigious New York University graduate filmmaking program at the Tisch School of the Arts. His student film *Tenacity* (1994), a short film and statement about tragedy along an empty reservation road, received wide critical attention that earned him a Rockefeller Foundation Intercultural Film/Video Fellowship to produce a narrative film.[29] He received an additional fellow-

Malinda Maynor, director of *Real Indian* (1997). Photograph by David Mehlman. Courtesy of the National Museum of the American Indian Film and Video Center.

ship to the Sundance Film Institute's script-writing workshop, where he began developing the screenplay for *This Is What It Means to Say Phoenix, Arizona,* based on the writings of Sherman Alexie (Coeur d'Alene/Spokane). Eyre received several financial awards based on that initial script that helped him and Alexie to complete their screenplay and seek funding to begin filming, which they received from ShadowCatcher Films in Seattle. After the film was completed, it was sold to Miramax Films in November 1997 and renamed *Smoke Signals*. At the 1998 Sundance Film Festival, the film received two top honors, the Audience Award and Filmmaker's Trophy.

▶

Our Tie with Aboriginal Production in Canada

Over a million people in Canada identify themselves as Aboriginal. The preexisting cultural ties among the Native peoples continues into the present despite Canadian and U.S. Indian policies imposed on them. The result of Indian policies in Canada have similarities with and major differences from that of U.S. Indian policies. The Dominion of Canada was established in 1867, at which time the federal government was constituted with responsibility for Indians and lands reserved for Indians. According to Canadian historian Robert J. Surtees, "the ultimate goal of the Canadian government was the achievement of enfranchisement."[30] As a result, suggests Surtees, autocratic and paternal Department of Indian Affairs agents became intimately involved in the local and private affairs of Indian bands.

Similarly, U.S. government Indian agents attempted to assimilate Indians, through boarding schools and by outlawing cultural and ritual practices, and these practices were enforced by later efforts to reorganize tribes with elected governments overseen by the Bureau of Indian Affairs. In the United States, but not in Canada, there were open declarations of war against Indian tribes, and there were far fewer opportunities for negotiation regarding land cessions and forced migration onto reservations.

Television broadcasting and filmmaking in Canada were grounded in official policy that provided early financial support by the Canadian government for Aboriginal production, which is particularly fascinating since no similar policy was ever established in the United States specifically for American Indians. Although the early support for Aboriginal production has since been reduced from initial funding levels, "Aboriginal broadcasting has contributed to both the distinctiveness of Canadian broadcasting and the democratization of the broadcasting system."[31]

In May 1967, the National Film Board of Canada was established by the Canadian Parliamentary government. Two years later, the National Film Board began a program called "Challenge for Change," a specific effort to train Aboriginal peoples to make films about themselves. The initial selection of Aboriginal participants required decisions about who among the Aboriginal people should receive the film training. The issue of diversity among Aboriginal and Native Americans is similar, but Canada also has geographic disparity, including vast tundra and the Arctic.

In 1969, the Telesat Canada Bill proposed a satellite system to provide television coverage and communication services to the northern Canadian territories, with the intention of bringing them into the Canadian mainstream. The Minister of Indian Affairs and a group called Northern Development lobbied the Canadian House of Commons for the passage of the satellite system. The Inuit and other First Nations in the region would be brought into the modern age by satellite communication.[32]

Anik was an early satellite project that did not allow for any reciprocal exchange. Programming was brought into Aboriginal communities with no way for them to share themselves with the rest of Canada. Anik restricted the flow of information by limiting broadcast times and requiring special licenses to broadcast, which prevented Aboriginal programs from being made. Broadcast opportunities for Aboriginal people were not forthcoming, though promised by the Canadian Broadcasting Corporation (CBC) for the Anik satellite. So Aboriginal communities in the North, with the assistance of Canadian field researchers, conducted their own study about the impact of mainstream television on Northern Aboriginal peoples. Inuit leaders used the data from the study, which revealed negative impacts of English programming in their communities, and challenged the Canadian government's cultural policy against broadcasting foreign language programs, which prevented culturally relevant programming being made available to them.[33] Their challenge resulted in the successful implementation of three satellite projects between 1976 and 1981: Naalakvik, Project Inukshuk, and Naalakvik II. These projects provided the technological infrastructure to link Inuit communities and train staff who began to experiment with programs specific to their community needs. By 1980, the Canadian Radio, Television, and Telecommunications Commission (CRTC) was convinced that the Inuit were competent to manage their own satellite programming and awarded a network license to the Inuit Broadcasting Corporation (IBC) in 1981. The IBC began operating five regional production centers and broadcast throughout Northern Quebec, Labrador, and the Northwest Territories for a minimum of seven hours per week, using the distribution services of the CBC Northern Service. In 1983, CBC satellite radio and television programs reached the remaining fifty-seven Inuit communities in the North. The Secretary of State Department of Canada implemented a Northern Broadcasting Policy (NBP) to control the funds associated with Aboriginal broadcasting, which insured that the CBC would continue to follow federal regulations.

Twenty years after the introduction of satellite television in the North, the history of the Inuit Broadcasting Corporation was documented in the film *Starting Fire with Gunpowder* (1991), directed by David Poisey and produced by William Hansen. The film presents some of the productions by the IBC and their use of documentary, drama, and animation to focus attention on issues important to the community, especially children's programs entirely in the Inuit language.

The Inuit Broadcasting Corporation was instrumental in training individuals such as Zacharias Kunuk. Kunuk was born in 1957 at Kapuivik in the Igloolik area of the Northwest Territories. He worked as an independent carver of Inuit sculpture for ten years before becoming a producer for the IBC in Igloolik. Since 1984, he has produced more than fifty videos in Inuktitut for satellite broadcast.[34] *Qaqqiq/Gathering Place* (1989) is one of his independent films about preindustrial Inuit life and involved members from Igloolik who reenacted their ancestral lifeways.

Aboriginal filmmakers are recognized for their talent for storytelling in their films. They have greatly benefited from government policies that financially support filmmakers in Canada. In 1990, the National Film Board of Canada created a film studio specifically for the purpose of assisting indigenous filmmakers. Studio One was launched in Edmonton, Alberta, and the National Film Board appointed Carol Geddes (Inland Tlingit) as a producer for the studio. It was intended that Studio One would assist film production by helping to write proposals for funding in addition to functioning as a studio by providing a facility and technical support where a film production could be based. Studio One was a major undertaking, requiring major capital to sustain itself—basically a good idea, but unrealistic. Geddes remained with Studio One for several years and eventually returned to filmmaking full-time. Her film *Picturing a People: George Johnston, Tlingit Photographer* (1997) is about George Johnston, whose photography prior to and after WWII is a visual history of events surrounding the changes affecting the Inland Tlingit.

In 1983, Canada's most celebrated Aboriginal filmmaker was Alanis Obomsawin (Abenaki), who received Canada's highest honor, an appointment to the Order of Canada, in recognition of her dedication to the preservation of the First Nations' cultural heritage through her filmmaking and activism.[35] Obomsawin began working in 1967 as a producer and director at the National Film Board of Canada. She continues to produce and direct films in addition to serving as staff director at the National Film Board in Montreal. In 1990, Obomsawin began filming her epic documentary, *Kanehsatake: 270 Years of Resistance* (1993), about the crisis surrounding an armed standoff between a group of Mohawks from the Kanawake Reserve and the Canadian National Guard. The Mohawks opposed the construction of a golf course expansion over an ancient Mohawk cemetery. The armed Mohawk resistance was provoked by the decision of the state and federal Canadian governments to send the army to remove the Mohawks from where they had barricaded themselves, which resulted in a seventy-eight day standoff. Obomsawin filmed the crisis from inside the Mohawk camp, and in the film she outlines the history of resistance by indigenous people in Canada and the censure of sovereign rights by the Canadian government. Obomsawin says, given our experience with oppression, "There had to be a document that came from us [Aboriginal people]. . . . people who watch TV all day long didn't have a sense of what really was happening there."[36] Two other films by Obomsawin are individual Mohawk stories about a woman and a man, participants in the resistance at Oka, *My Name Is Kahentiiosa* (1995) and *Spudwrench—Kahnawake Man* (1997).[37]

Filmmaking has reconnected Aboriginal and Native Americans in new ways. It has been responsible for bringing us into contact with other in-

Kanehsatake: 270 Years of Resistance (1993), director/producer Alanis Obomsawin. Courtesy of the Photo Library of the National Film Board of Canada. Copyright National Film Board of Canada. All rights reserved.

digenous peoples. *Storytellers of the Pacific* (1996) is a four-part series that documents the experiences of indigenous people with regard to their experience of colonization and the continuance and survival of their cultures. The series highlights the shared stories of Aborigines in Australia, Native Hawaiians, Maori in New Zealand, Chamoru in Guam, Seri in Mexico, Samoans, Alaskan Aleut, Northwest Coast Indians, California Indians, and Inuits in Canada. Frank Blythe and Lurlaine McGregor served as executive producers. Blythe is the executive director of Native American Public Telecommunications, and McGregor was the executive director of Pacific Islanders in Communications (PIC) and is currently the executive director of 'Olelo, the Corporation for Community Television in Hawai'i.

Pacific Islanders in Communications was founded in Hawai'i in 1991. It is funded by the Corporation for Public Broadcasting as a nonprofit national media organization. PIC has increased the visibility of Pacific Islanders in public television programming through the production of programs made by and about Pacific Islanders and their cultures that increases sensitivity about them.[38] The organization has produced over twenty major programs for television broadcast, held numerous training workshops in production, and encouraged extensive community involvement and outreach in their productions.

A unique reference to documenting indigenous cultures by its own members comes from the Maori expression used in storytelling: "Children, welcome to your past." The invitation is to learn about your history from the people who preserved it for you, your grandmothers and grandfathers. The context of watching a film made by your own people is novel, since until very recently indigenous cultures have not been self-portrayed, but at the same time, it is continuous with a long tradition of learning through intergenerational storytelling.

[5]   *On the Road to* Smoke Signals

When Chris Eyre sat in the director's chair for *Smoke Signals* in 1998, he was the first Native American to direct a major release feature film since Edwin Carewe's brief career ended in the 1920s. *Smoke Signals,* distributed by Miramax, premiered at the 1998 Sundance Film Festival, where it received the Filmmaker's Trophy and the Audience Award. The elite film audiences there who voted for the Native American film, and the support for the film by a major distributor, have helped to reposition Native American participation in filmmaking.

Eyre's success fulfilled a prophesy made by Steve Lewis (Lakota/ Tohono O'odham) at the 1993 Imagining Indians: Native American Film and Video Festival:

> I think it's only a matter of time before our generation gets the expertise and a story that we can go with, that we can possibly turn into a small, all-Indian, independent feature. I don't think it's going to come from a big studio hiring an Indian director, that's not too realistic. One of the more exciting parts of Indian film and video now are the young people who could possibly make a serious change in the next maybe four or five years—a media change.[1]

The production of *Smoke Signals* demonstrated that American Indians can make a good commercial product while telling a good story with Indians as the central characters. For too long, Native Americans have been viewed as activists and positioned as opponents of mainstream white filmmakers. Because we have not been privy to the feature filmmaking industry that is Hollywood, too much attention has been given to our advocating against a mindset that has precluded full Indian participation in filmmaking since its inception.

The struggle for Native Americans to break into mainstream filmmaking is captured by Sandra Osawa's response to a question during an

Evan Adams, foreground, and Adam Beach in *Smoke Signals* (1997), coproducer/
writer Sherman Alexie, director Chris Eyre. Photograph courtesy of Miramax Films.

interview in 1993. The reporter had asked her to respond to the comments
of Michael Apted, film director of *Thunderheart* (1992), who had said
that he believed that there would never be an Indian director in the United
States due to the infrastructure there. Osawa responded, "Well, it's not the
infrastructure. . . . I believe it has something to do with racism."[2] The irony
for Native Americans is that we must overcome the negative and incorrect
identity that was in part created by the film industry in order to make our
own films.

But time heals some wounds, and as more time goes by we have more
reason for hope. Casey Camp Horinek (Ponca) said at the 1994 Imagining
Indians: Native American Film and Video Festival: "When you look back
twenty years ago, when the media blitzes were on Wounded Knee, and you
think about a time ten years ago when we weren't getting our voices heard
in virtually any way. . . . Look at five years ago, four years ago, and three
years ago. . . . Now look to the future. . . . Look to 2010 and that next generation because they're going to be doing what we're doing, only better."[3]
The beauty of Native storytelling is when one story ends, another begins.

In this chapter I discuss six films and videos that preceded *Smoke
Signals*. These films, all by Native Americans, set the stage for Eyre's film
and represent the struggle by Native Americans to overcome the visual
genocide and to reimagine and revisualize what it means to be an Indian.
The films are Victor Masayesva Jr.'s *Hopiit, Lighting the 7th Fire* by Sandra
Osawa, *Navajo Talking Picture* by Arlene Bowman, *High Horse* by Randy

Victor Masayesva Jr., "Imagining Indians" (1994). Masayesva was artistic director of the 1994 Imagining Indians: Native American Film and Video Festival, Scottsdale, Arizona. Reproduced by permission of the artist.

Redroad, *Hands of History* by Loretta Todd, and my own *A Video Book*. I selected these productions in an attempt to reflect diversity in tribal affiliation and subject matter, originality of production, and their contributions to the Native American filmmaking movement.

▶————————————————————————————————————

Hopiit (1982), Dir. Victor Masayesva Jr., IS Productions

In 1983, just as I was beginning my own filmmaking studies at the Anthropology Film Center in Santa Fe, I attended a screening of *Hopiit* at the Institute of American Indian Arts Museum. *Hopiit*, a sixteen-minute video, was Victor Masayesva Jr.'s directorial debut. It is about the daily activities at a Hopi village within the cycle of a year. The activities Masayesva attends to with the camera are an outgrowth of natural rhythms in the community of which he has made a careful and quiet study. It was—and remains—inspiring to watch seemingly simple activities appear so valuable.

Hopiit begins outdoors with the gentle movement of prayer feathers, imparting good will to the viewers. A deep blue fills the sky, and the voice of an elderly man speaking Hopi is barely audible as his shadow comes into view. Dramatically, the camera moves slowly from the shadow to the man, seated by a window, who then looks out the window toward the sky. The elder is telling what sounds like a very old story. The view of the sun is dispersed by an image of a buffalo dancer's headdress appearing through a gray screen, an illusion created with video editing technology. The abstraction of the dancer is more suggestive of a buffalo spirit than of a dancer's performance. Masayesva's symbolic opening becomes the entry point to the daily cycles of Hopi.

A man carrying a load of wood tied on his back with a trade blanket is seen making his way in a winter blizzard. We hear the wailing storm, and a dog's barking is quieted with a transition indoors where a group of women are weaving baskets. A very young child about four years old intently watches the women weave their baskets. Masayesva captures the moment with close-ups of the weaving without fixing any attention on the gaze of the child, and so avoids distracting the child. The contrast between the storm outside and the feeling of security indoors is represented by several generations of women quietly talking and joking among themselves as they weave. The scene captures how young children learn how to make baskets through observation.

As a transition to the next scene, the sound of children's laughter is heard. The children come into view and are seen playing on sleds—typifying the joy of children. A close scrutiny will reveal that the "sled" is actually a metal drawer from a desk like those found in a government office. Slowly, the camera reveals the wide-open spaces where the children are playing, as the focus shifts to a white horse running in the distance. The camera blurs, and there is a change to the village and smoke rising from a chimney.

In the next scene Masayesva presents a Deer Dance, which is usually performed during the winter ceremonial cycle. The deer-horn headdresses worn by the young dancers display an abundant use of evergreen branches. In my earliest memories of participating in ceremonial dances in my Pueblo community, holding evergreen branches in my hands is symbolic of everlasting life. Watching any Native dance is best experienced by listening to the song as you watch the dancers become the spirit of the animal or story they are telling. The Deer Dance is performed as a homage to deer who give themselves as food. By wearing the deer horns, the dancer becomes the spirit of the deer.

Masayesva completes the winter season with scenes of a snowstorm followed by a woman's song in Hopi. The image of delicate flower blossoms announce spring's arrival. A cut is made indoors to a woman who is preparing blue corn cakes while we hear and see spring winds sweep the ground outside, creating sand dunes. Another scene is of a farmer using a digging stick to make holes in the sandy, moist soil, in which he sows seeds. The camera's position allows us to see the farmer's hands work with the earth. Masayesva successfully brings a unique quality of olfactory perception into the video by using images that suggest the smell of earth.

There is a cut to an eagle chained on a rooftop and feeding on a piece of meat. In spite of being chained, the eagle appears to belong there, yet not in a captive way. The eagle is a celebrated bird and the source of many stories, but it is not a pet. The significance of the eagle, and all birds, particularly among the Hopi, is a respectful relationship rooted in their origins and ceremonial life. Federal and state government restrictions on religious and ceremonial use of eagle feathers and other birds of prey that are endangered species weighs heavily on the religious freedom rights of American Indians; thus, Masayesva's documentation of the eagle on a rooftop demonstrates the Hopis' self-determined action regarding such federal regulation.[4]

There is a transition from the roof to the ground where two young boys target practice with child-sized handmade bows and arrows. Imitating their fathers and uncles while having fun in play, they are actually preparing themselves for hunting when they grow older.

The sound of thunder from an approaching storm can be heard, and an extreme long camera view shows lightning and dark rain clouds. A rain shower is captured in a cornfield as a transition to a close-up of mature corn plants gives way to a blur of sunlight on corn leaves that glitter with

Victor Masayesva Jr. receives the 1995 Maya Deren Award from the American Film Institute; Beverly R. Singer, presenter. Photograph courtesy of the American Film Institute, Los Angeles.

the spirit of life. We hear Hopi spoken as the camera fixes on a close-up of ladybugs mating. It is an outstandingly subtle and distinct image of procreation and the same process that takes place among corn plants and humans.

The camera shifts to follow a woman with an armful of freshly picked corn and then to a child running barefoot through the cornfield. Masayesva cuts to a dance at the village. The headpieces worn by the women are made of brightly painted wood with corn, butterflies, and other nature symbols. In contrast to the women's headpieces, the male dancer has a single feather tied to his hair. The Corn Dance is held as thanksgiving to the corn that sustains life and retells the story of the corn's growth that springs from seeds planted in the earth, aided by the rain that helps them grow.

After the dance sequence, Masayesva turns our attention to tasks being completed by a group of young boys who are having fun emptying a truckload of dried white corn. There is a cut to the last scene, of an older woman quietly stacking corn in a recessed niche in her home. A very effective pull-back dolly shot reveals a wall of blue corn neatly stacked in rolls.

Hopiit compels the viewer to identify subtly. Masayesva captures Hopi tending to their daily tasks without questioning their motives. The video affirms that an ordinary life is the most fulfilling one. *Hopiit* seems longer than its screening time of sixteen minutes, the result of Masayesva's cinematic attention to detail and Hopi timing, a sensibility that contrasts with a modern attention span, which is unusually short.

Interestingly, although no time frame is established in *Hopiit,* it is clear that it is contemporary. The film has an essay quality in which the people featured are neither distracted by the camera nor show any concern with its presence; instead, they provide a sense of constancy throughout the production and continue to give full attention to what they are doing. These are not mysterious activities, either. Masayesva's sequences of dance, song, ritual, ceremony, and the profane tasks are associated with their appropriate season.

Masayesva's portrayal of his community calls to my mind the views of American Indian anthropologist Alfonso Ortiz (Tewa), who has since retired to the spirit world, but who will be remembered for sharing his unique anthropological perspective. With regard to Eurocentric perceptions of Indians, he wrote:

> Indeed, when we contemplate how Indian people have been defined in American history, as uncouth, devil-worshipping savages who had no proper notions of law or government and who, moreover, kept putting themselves on the wrong side of the frontier, one has to wonder just how they managed to survive during the thousands of years before Europeans came over to rescue them from their miserable condition.[5]

Hopiit is visible evidence of indigenous cultural continuance and survival.

▶ ───────────────────────────────────────

Lighting the 7th Fire (1994), Dir. Sandra Osawa, Upstream Productions

Lighting the 7th Fire is a video about the Chippewa and the spearfishing controversy in northern Wisconsin that unleashed racist attacks by whites opposed to Indian fishing rights. American Indian treaties were legally determined by U.S. courts early in the nineteenth century. The knowledge of Indian treaties are a cornerstone in American history that was dismissed from public education with the hope that "Indians" would disappear. When the Chippewa began reasserting their cultural rights and practices, they were met with angry resistance among whites who organized racist anti-Indian campaigns to prevent them from pursuing their traditional spearfishing practices.

The Chippewa honor a prophesy that speaks of seven fires representing seven periods of time, which Osawa evokes with the title *Lighting the 7th Fire.* The prophesy states that the sixth fire was the time of great hardship that followed the dismantling of Chippewa culture and practices after the arrival of whites. At the opening of Osawa's production, a beaded floral pattern familiar in Chippewa art is used as a background to display the seventh fire prophesy that tells of "a return to traditional ways as a sign that the seventh fire is beginning."[6]

Osawa establishes the opening sequence with a Chippewa prayer by a spiritual leader. At the conclusion of the prayer, we hear the singing of crickets in a forest, then there is a cut to a Chippewa spearfishing in a boat on a lake in the dark. There is a close-up of a speared walleye being put in a bucket in the boat. We hear the voice of a young woman: "We're not against the Indians; we just want equal rights. We're not against them, but they're killing all the fish, so what's next?" We see the young woman among a group of protesters making victory signs. Then we hear other white protesters yelling, "Equal rights, equal rights." We see spotlights that expose a group of protesters along a fence, men, women, and children, who are yelling, "Timber nigger, timber nigger." Two signs carried by the protesters read, "1 Nation under God" and "Every Race In The World Lives In America Under One Law, Except Res. Indians." The meaning of the signs may not be clear to those not familiar with the myriad of circumstances surrounding the Chippewa, who in the mid-1970s began asserting a legal right to fish in lakes off their reservation.

Nick Hockings appears throughout the program, connecting his personal experiences as a Chippewa spearfisher with the larger Chippewa

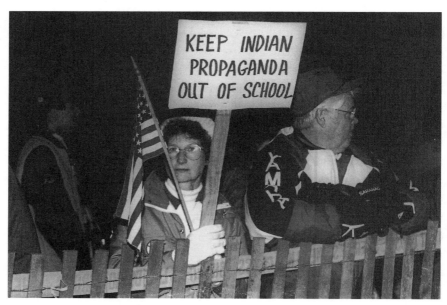

Lighting the 7th Fire (1994), producer/director Sandra Osawa. Photograph courtesy of Upstream Productions.

story in statements such as "spearfishing is something that has taken place for centuries."

There is a cut to a sign: "Welcome to Lac du Flambeau," which is ironic in light of the controversy. Osawa takes the time in the video to explain that French fur trappers gave the village its name, which means "Lake of the Flames," after observing Chippewa in canoes with torches spearing for fish in the lake. Paintings by early American artist Paul Kane are shown, which depict a historical image of Chippewa spearfishing from canoes with torches attached. Nick Hockings personalizes the Chippewa story when he says, "Our ancestors sat in these meetings and had to make hard decisions; they paid a heavy price for us to be on these lakes." Hockings explains that a court decision, known as the Gurnoe Decision of 1973, acknowledged the Chippewa right to spearfish off the reservation. He says that the warrior spirit of older Chippewa who risked everything to retain their rights to spearfish had been vindicated. Newspaper clippings and court documents are shown that explain the significance of the Gurnoe Decision. The Chippewa Treaty of 1854, permitting the Red Lake and Bad River Chippewas to fish, hunt, and gather on ceded Chippewa lands is displayed.

The video cuts to the home of one of the Tribble brothers. Fred Tribble says in an interview, "Our elders retained the right to fish and hunt. They were always thinking about the future." The camera cuts to Mike Tribble who says, "It was like a light being turned on." Fred Tribble recalls that he and his brother went fishing off the reservation after the Gurnoe Decision, in 1974, and were arrested by a Wisconsin state game warden. He showed a copy of the Chippewa treaty to the warden, who ignored it. The Tribbles filed a suit against the state of Wisconsin, and nine years later, in 1983, they won their court case, which affirmed their rights to spearfish off the reservation. Fred Tribble says, "I thought about our elders who couldn't do what was their right, about us who can do it now, and about the future, too."

The story shifts to an interview with Ike Gokee, a Chippewa elder from Red Cliff, who recalls his fear while hunting in his youth: "A lot of times, I'd be in the grass hiding, afraid to move." Early photographs demonstrate the commercial exploitation of timber and copper after Wisconsin became a state. Statistical details are presented in words that say the state of Wisconsin issued 925,000 fishing licenses to non-Indians in 1960, and a montage of photographs depicts the growth of tourism dependent on fishing and hunting in northern Wisconsin, underscored by Louis Armstrong's rendition of "Gone Fishing."

The interview continues with Ike Gokee, who remembers when food was so scarce he ate lard on bread with salt and pepper "to make it taste different." His eyes reveal a distant sadness, and gratitude perhaps, for having survived the past. A photograph of him and his deceased wife, Victoria, show them in a fond embrace. In words over the image, it is revealed that Ike and Victoria Gokee were instrumental in retaining the fishing rights for the Red Cliff and Bad River Chippewa, who forced the Gurnoe decision in 1973. Osawa uses the opportunity to reach further into Chippewa history and tell how John Blackbird was arrested and served thirty days of hard labor for fishing. Blackbird appealed to the U.S. District Court, which later affirmed the Chippewa right to fish in 1901.

The story cuts to 1985 when growing numbers of Chippewa began spearfishing off the reservation. We see newspaper headlines that read "2,000 Protesters at Anti-Indian Treaty Rally," and we hear protesters shouting, "Bullshit, bullshit." Other protesters' signs read "Keep Indian Propaganda out of Schools." The insertion of home video that recorded anti-Chippewa protests dating back to April 1990 is effectively used to illustrate the hostile environment at the start of the controversy.

White protesters are seen along roadways in the dark during a snowstorm waving American flags. Bill Means of the International Indian Treaty Council is interviewed about their participation in the Chippewa community. He shares that the council was called in to protect Chippewa women and children at boat landings because the sports fisherman were getting more aggressive, showering people with beer and rocks. Means describes how they walked through the white protesters with a traditional drum with no incident, which for him demonstrated the "amazing power of the drum."

Osawa's production is one of the first programs of its kind to openly expose anti-Indian sentiment and racist protests by whites, which are not limited to Wisconsin and also persist in other parts of the country, but which are noticeably absent in productions by whites about "Indians."

In an interview, community scholar and advocate Walter Bressette (Red Cliff Chippewa) speaks about the reaction in Wisconsin after the 1973 Gurnoe decision:

> No one in the State of Wisconsin was prepared academically, intellectually, for the court ruling. Everyone acted as though the judges in Chicago gave to the Chippewa, out of thin air, special rights, when in fact the Chippewa court ruling was consistent with a long series of court decisions.

Bressette recalls the Wisconsin Natural Resources Department spokesman saying, the day after the federal court decision, that "the only thing left after the Chippewa are done will be water skiing." Emotionally charged misinformation, suggests Bressette, was used to cultivate racism that prompted organized protests sponsored by groups such as Protect American Rights and Resources (PARR) and Stop Treaty Abuse. The latter group produced a beer to raise funds for their anti-Indian campaign. (Sadly, Bresette passed to the spirit world in 1999 at the age of fifty-one.)

An interview with Larry Peterson, a representative of Protect American Rights and Resources, says he believes "the Chippewa have been given a court license to steal" that, in his opinion, will affect the overall economy. The film cuts to Bill Means, representing the American Indian Treaty Council, who says that national television news showed that the violence in Wisconsin was clearly being committed by whites and that is what led to a reduction in tourism, not the Chippewa court decision itself.

An interview with Jim Schendler, a representative of the Indian Fishing Commission, adds another perspective about the state's fishing economy. He points out that environmental pollution, including mercury contamination, fertilizer, faulty septic systems, and similar developments, has reduced the walleye population in Wisconsin. Schendler refers to a report released in 1979 by the state Natural Resource Department indicating the need to limit the fishing of walleye. In 1987, the Natural Resource Department in Wisconsin appears to have used the Tribbles' court victory to enforce the limit of two walleye fish per fisherman in the state. This suggests the Chippewa were used as scapegoats, although Schendler does not say that in his interview.

There is a transition to Hockings at his home, where he is preparing his fishing gear. He shares information about his fishing helmet, in which a headlight from a car is used and charged by a car battery. The car headlight replaced the old torches used in the past by Chippewa fishermen in canoes, but the intent is the same: "As we motor along [in the boat], we can look into the water and we can see the eyes of the fish." The cultural significance of spearfishing is revealed by this comment. His reference to being able to "see the eyes of the fish" before it is speared is an extraordinary observation. Because the walleye were a primary food source for the Chippewa, seeing the eyes allows for a moment of thanksgiving, a connection with the fish whose life you are taking for your survival. The moment prior to spearing the fish is a sacred moment between the Chippewa and the fish and one that has been repeated for centuries.

The Chippewa spearfishing controversy is the source of many stories that Osawa gives care and attention to. In an interview with Nick Hockings and his wife, they provide dramatic details about the attempt by the state of Wisconsin to pay fifty million dollars secretly to the Chippewa Tribal Council in exchange for the Chippewa to cede hunting and fishing rights. The state's offer was made public and the Chippewa Tribal Council decided to have a vote referendum about the state's deal that tribal members defeated.

A transition is made to explore the impact on children. Nick Hockings visited schools as part of a program he participated in to share Chippewa culture and history. At one elementary school, he says, a boy asked Hockings, "Do you Indians still kill cowboys and eat them?" Hockings asks, "What if that young boy grows up to be a lawyer, a federal judge, or a senator?" We learn that the perpetuation of negative stereotypes of "Indians" is alive and well in public education.

In an interview with Eugene Begay, Red Cliff Chippewa spiritual leader, he describes a Water Ceremony he led at the request of the Lac du Flambeau Chippewa. He speaks about the water spirits as real beings who receive the prayer offerings. He recalls the use of a sacred pipe and says that "our sacrifice was accepted, and acknowledged all life. We prayed for non-Indian people to have understanding."

A cut to Nick Hockings is made. He shares his belief that "Our water spirits are some of the strongest spirits that we have. We offer things to that water—tobacco, prayers, and pieces of clothing." Hockings is shown preparing his boat for fishing as we hear him say, "Every court case we won, it was because of the pipe."

Osawa begins to bring some closure. Statements by Tom Maulson, Lac du Flambeau tribal president, describe how his life was changed as the result of the controversy. He says it taught him about himself as he started listening to elders, using the pipe, and listening to his people. Another statement is made by Andy Gokee, grandson of Ike Gokee, who says, "It was prophesied that our people would go through a hard time, and then there would be a reemergence of these things when Indian people would live and prosper."

There is a cut to a motorboat gliding slowly in a lake at dawn. We hear Nick Hockings in a voice-over: "It's a strong feeling knowing your ancestors traveled this way, so being able to do as our ancestors have done, this is who we are as a people."

Osawa's use of Chippewa oral tradition carries significant importance to this story, and because it is the foundation upon which they retell their story to retain their right to spearfish, it becomes a story for the next generation. Osawa's production also honors their story by invoking the Chippewa prophesy.

The history and controversies involving Native Americans are the direct result of events that threaten ideals of American democracy. But Osawa treats the controversy with respect by not ignoring the history that is usually left to conjecture. *Lighting the 7th Fire* provides a solution to understanding Native perspectives and the oral tradition that demonstrates how sharing what happened is healing.

▶

Navajo Talking Picture (1984), Dir. Arlene Bowman

Navajo Talking Picture is a painfully honest film portrait by Arlene Bowman. She employs the filmmaking process to reunite with her Navajo relatives from whom she was separated at the age of six when her parents left
the reservation and relocated to Phoenix. Bowman's opening narration explains that while in art school she decided to make a film about her grandmother, Ann Bila. Assuming that her grandmother would agree to be in
her film, she travels to the Navajo reservation with a camera crew, only to
learn that her grandmother is not willing to be filmed.

Bowman's desire to make the film with her grandmother intensifies,
and she attempts to get her grandmother's support through an interpreter.
Because Bowman does not speak Navajo, she is unable to explain, much
less convince, her grandmother to work with her. At times, it is difficult to
watch the invasive camera that appears to stalk the grandmother. Bowman's
use of an interpreter in mixing the film's sound track is very effective,
making it possible to understand her grandmother's responses about not
wanting to appear in Bowman's film. We sense and feel her grandmother's
growing insecurity and frustration with her granddaughter who appears
oblivious to her grandmother's desire to be left alone.

Bowman's personal story is interwoven throughout the film, which
illuminates the enormous cultural distance between her and her relatives
on the reservation. Bowman cannot accept her grandmother's opposition
to being filmed. Bowman's film is a testament to the fact that Native people
have ways of seeing, believing, and doing things that modern society often
cannot or will not accept.

Upon Bowman's arrival at the Navajo reservation with her camera
crew, the initial introduction between Bowman and her grandmother is
friendly. Through an interpreter she learns that her grandmother does not
want to be filmed. Bowman continues the shooting despite her grandmother's resistance, and her grandmother becomes less cooperative with
Bowman. She ignores Bowman's questions that the interpreter asks. In
frustration, Bowman turns to her film crew (whom we never see on camera) and says, "What's the use?" We are privy to hear the interpreter repeat
what her grandmother says, "I'm angry with you," referring to the continued filming by Bowman.

Bowman films her grandmother butchering a sheep and talks with
admiration about her grandmother as a strong, independent woman, as
if speaking about herself as well. With the camera she follows her grandmother shopping at a local trading post. Bowman uses the opportunity to

describe life on the reservation as harsh and isolated in contrast to her life in the city, which she perceives as more convenient. Bowman attends a family gathering and continues filming. The gathering is also attended by her grandmother. Afterward, Bowman returns with her camera to her grandmother's home.

At this point in the film there is a visible change in the grandmother's body posture. Her grandmother keeps her back to the camera and appears agitated by the camera and Bowman's presence. In one scene, her grandmother attempts to flee the room where she's being filmed, and the film tension increases also. Visibly upset, Bowman says to her film crew, "I don't have anything else to say to her." Bowman goes into the room where her grandmother is sitting on a bed, her face downward, looking at a magazine as though she is reading. As soon as Bowman enters, her grandmother awkwardly twists her body to keep from being filmed. Bowman's grandmother speaks Navajo to Bowman, which is translated for viewers: "Well, when I was young, my grandmother told us stories. I was given stories in my prayers. To this day I remember that, and I was not told my grandchild would take pictures of me." This is a turning point in the story as Bowman turns the camera on herself and begins to share her personal odyssey about her obsession to learn from her grandmother.

We see Bowman in a playful moment inside the sheep pen at her grandmother's where she chases a lamb and tries to catch it; the irony of this scene is profound in its reflection of Bowman similarly pursuing her grandmother. Then we see Bowman preparing to leave the reservation. She is seen saying goodbye to her grandmother and handing her a folded wad of money. Her grandmother simply accepts it. Bowman asks through the interpreter in the scene if her grandmother resents the fact that she doesn't speak Navajo. The interpreter gives her grandmother's response: "Yes, very hard to communicate because we can't talk to each other."

The film takes us to Los Angeles in a scene with freeways and then to Bowman's apartment. There is a cut to Bowman at school where she reviews her film footage of the reservation. In a voice-over she speaks about her decision to include herself in her film. Her initial approach was undermined at the reservation, but Bowman remains unwilling to accept the fact that her grandmother does not want to be filmed. She seeks the advice of a Native American student counselor at the university and asks his opinion about her grandmother's refusal to work with her. It is not clear if the counselor has seen Bowman's footage; his response to Bowman's question is very general, in which he refers to a fear of the camera among some Native people.

Bowman confers with her mother about her film and her grandmother's

Navajo Talking Picture (1984), producer/director Arlene Bowman. Photograph courtesy of Women Make Movies, New York.

refusal to be filmed. Bowman's mother says that people on the reservation are just different, which I interpret as difficult to understand.

Bowman returns to the Navajo reservation and arrives unexpectedly. She looks for an interpreter, and finding one, asks him to explain to her grandmother that the film is about Bowman. Her grandmother remains firm in her original decision: "I don't want to be in it." Owing to film processing or her grandmother's energy, there appears to be a halo or aura of light around the older woman that keeps her distanced from Bowman. Bowman continues to provide interpretation of her grandmother's words: "Doesn't she have any pride? . . . Why does she keep following me around like that? . . . That's enough," referring to Bowman's filming.

On her third trip to the reservation, she finds no change in her grandmother's position. Bowman leaves almost immediately and returns to Los Angeles. In my opinion, it is a good decision. The film concludes with Bowman driving, looking out at the road ahead. She turns her head to her companions, presumably the film crew, and asks, "What do you think, guys? I want some reaction." In a voice-over, Bowman says, "Understanding is what I want, understanding between my grandmother and myself and myself and the Navajo."

Bowman's story is not contemplative, nor is it an ordinary film. It is Bowman's own story performance as a novice filmmaker that is noteworthy in her determination to complete this film. Her inability to communicate with her grandmother in spite of the help she received from a Navajo interpreter, in the final analysis, suggests a major rupture in Bowman's personal cultural understanding.

Navajo Talking Picture is like watching a crusade by an outsider who clumsily attempts to reestablish ties with strangers who are supposed to be her extended family. Her severity at times in her pursuit to film her grandmother, ignoring her grandmother's request not to be filmed, cannot be dismissed easily. The story contains important lessons, especially for younger Native Americans, who, like Bowman, have had little contact with relatives who reside at the reservation where, in this case, Navajo is spoken primarily by the elders, although that has changed significantly since Bowman's film was released. With the deaths of elders who spoke the indigenous language fluently, English is becoming more predominant. It is a major concern among Native tribes that, with the loss of Native language skills, the communication of cultural knowledge and information is compromised by the use of English concepts and words that do not express their actual or true meaning.

Bowman's initial return to the reservation for the purpose of making a film appears to outweigh a personal desire to become acquainted with her family. In 1983, as the result of completing this film, however, Bowman became the first Navajo woman to earn an M.F.A. in filmmaking at the University of California at Los Angeles.

Bowman's personal lack of sensitivity and disrespect for her grandmother's privacy is a major departure from general rules of conduct in Native families that typically require children to have respect for elders. In this case, in spite of Bowman's blood relationship with her grandmother, she is a stranger from the outset and remains so throughout.

Midway into the film, Bowman's grandmother extends herself as a grandmother to a grandchild and tells how she was told stories, which are prayers in themselves. The grandmother goes on to say that these stories were told to her by her grandmother, and that nowhere in her memory is there a mention of picture taking while telling these stories. I contend that Bowman's grandmother believed that because cameras were not associated with cultural survival, cameras were of no interest to her. Furthermore, her grandmother is also suggesting that cameras were especially inappropriate for Navajo storytelling, since Navajo stories are private matters and hallowed. The information Bowman's grandmother told her came from her memory of teachings by Bowman's great-great-grandmother. Bowman's grandmother wanted her granddaughter to honor these teachings. Bowman offers no response to this, which leads me to believe that she was not aware of the significance of her grandmother's explanation, at least not at the time of shooting her film. The sense of bewilderment is apparent as Bowman's grandmother is unable to defend herself against the camera. It is reminiscent also of history when Native people were unable to defend themselves against white encroachment. Bowman's grandmother appears to be in her seventies; in her youth she would have heard stories about the campaign against the Navajo and of the "Navajo Long Walk."[7]

As heard in her film's commentary, Bowman appears to have little awareness of, understanding for, or patience with Navajo culture. The open display of conflict between Bowman and her grandmother will strongly affect viewers from any walk of life. The result of being alienated from the Navajo social structure leads Bowman to comment near the end of her film, "I'm not doing a bad thing," meaning perhaps that she did not intend to upset and hurt her grandmother's feelings. Bowman never concedes defeat, nor does she acknowledge her own personal feelings about being rejected by her grandmother and her aunt. In the film, Bowman shares a letter written by her aunt telling her that she was not welcome back to her grandmother's home and shames Bowman for not being able to speak Navajo. The private matter of the Bowman family's decision to leave the reservation is not entirely clear in the film either. We must be sensitive to Bowman's personal trials in her feeling of rejection by her extended family residing at the reservation. This, too, may explain her need to vehemently pursue making this film. It makes sense that at the end of the film Bowman seeks approval from her film crew, but the approval and acceptance she covets must come from her own people. The inherent value of watching Arlene Bowman's story is to begin a dialogue among Natives about our cultural understanding and use of our indigenous tongues and our hopes for the future.

▶

High Horse (1994), Dir. Randy Redroad, Third World Newsreel

High Horse is a story about the metropolis of New York City, where immigrant and indigenous spirits are connected to their dislocated history. Redroad's portrait of a handful of Native Americans in New York City resembles the individual experiences of approximately forty thousand Native Americans who reside in the metropolitan New York City area.[8] Redroad's story mirrors his life as a bike messenger for three of the eight years he lived in New York between the mid-1980s and early 1990s. The film distributor,

Third World Newsreel, describes *High Horse* as "a provocative narrative film exploring the concept of 'home' for Native Americans." *High Horse* opens in what the filmmaker calls the "artificial world of the Colonizers," a modern American city. "From a cop to a young bike messenger, dislocated Native People search for and sometimes find their figurative—and literal—homes. They reclaim what has been stolen from the past in different journeys of loss, love, and identity."[9]

Redroad's humor begins with his reference to the film being "a random headdress production" and "a freedom myth," both disqualifiers. A gray-haired Native American sleeping on a park bench wakes to the sound of voices. Male voice says, "Isn't it amazing what man can do." A New York City skyline comes into view; aboard a boat is a white couple, a woman and her partner. She comments, "It's [the skyline] beautiful. . . . they look like big silver redwoods." Her partner responds, "Yeah, they sold it for about twenty bucks worth of beads. . . . no head for business, I guess." New York City is a legendary place where "Indians" figure in a remarkable early American cultural myth faithfully repeated today that says Indians who occupied the island of Manhattan in the seventeenth century either bartered, exchanged, or sold the island to European immigrants for what amounted to twenty-four dollars. The legend appeared in my middle school history book and probably in every other school history lesson as well.[10]

Redroad's own guitar playing creates a musical score that contrasts with New York's fast-paced public persona. Sitting in a tent on his apartment floor, Redroad is learning Cherokee from audiotapes. In English: "From where do they come from." The Native man rises from the park bench and continues to hear voices. The English translation repeats: "Hello . . . good morning." We glimpse Redroad's personal wit, which effectively drew my attention to Native idiosyncrasies such as the headless Pilgrim figure on a table in his apartment.

Native Americans by and large accept the presence of a spiritual world that runs parallel to our daily life, although many people prefer not to discuss these beliefs openly because of the popular appropriation of them. Paula Gunn Allen in her coveted book *The Sacred Hoop* affirms that spirit is real: "Over the years I have located the following major themes or issues that pertain to American Indians. . . . Indians and spirits are always found together."[11] Redroad immediately connects us to his Cherokee ancestry in two ways: first, through the spirit figure in the guise of an older homeless Native American in New York City, and second, through his incorporation of Cherokee words and phrases that serve as transitions through the film. Redroad's storytelling works as an organic whole. The combination of people, events, and ideas, while meant to be a narrative, are from actual experiences of urban Indians.

In another part of the city, a young adult Native American male with long flowing hair stands in obvious distress outside an apartment building, looking up at a window. A young Native woman with a fishing pole over her shoulder walks next to her boyfriend, a white male in a business suit. They kiss and go their separate ways. A policeman on horseback rides by and takes notice of the young man in distress outside the apartment building. Exiting from a different apartment building is an African-American couple, the young man with a bicycle in tow; the couple hug and part in opposite directions.

A cut is made to the African-American male who just left his partner in an embrace; he says "shit" after making a phone call. We see a messenger service office, which explains his dismay with no bicycle messages to deliver. A cut is made to a typical city diner, where we see Redroad eating breakfast as he repeats words in Cherokee to himself. Seated next to him are two men of color talking about a friend who was jailed for drumming in the park. A policeman enters the diner and orders coffee to go as the conversations continue.

The men who were at the diner are shown in the park with drums where they continue their conversation. One of the men says, "You got to go and take it. . . . whatever you need in life to survive, you have to go and claim that food, clothing, shelter." Sitting in the same park and gazing out aimlessly at the world is the young African-American woman by herself. The suggestion in the film is that people should go and claim their place in the world instead of sitting and waiting for it to come to them, as it never will on its own.

The white couple previously on the boat look at a monument depicting an "Indian" in Plains Indian regalia receiving a strand of beads from a man in a helmet of European origin. The husband takes a photograph of his wife by the monument. The camera moves in to show the inscription on the monument, which reads: "April 22, 1625, the Fort Amsterdam Chamber of the West Indian Company purchased Manhattan and laid the foundation of the City of New York." After we hear the husband read the monument description, we hear him say "wow," which is drowned out by African-sounding drumming.

The American flag is hoisted up on a pole in the park as we hear the Cherokee word for "sisters." We see the African-American woman using the park bench to exercise and stretch while the Native woman fishes with her pole in a stagnant pond. The film's tempo moves to a crawl as we hear the words "I am hungry," spoken as if to imply that something is about to happen. The African-American bicycle messenger rides by a food delivery bicyclist who is white and steals a white bag from the bicycle basket. New Yorkers familiar with deli service would notice that the bag is from one of the expensive delis in the city. In the bag is one raw fish and some bananas.

The film cuts back to the young man with the flowing hair, who shouts angrily from outside at an apartment window: "I don't want to be Indian, but I'm proud of it. . . . I love you." His words echo the mixed-up pride he feels about being "Indian" and also the resignation of self-defeat. The mounted policeman calls for a police car. The police car arrives, and he is handcuffed after resisting and struggling with the police. One of the police refers to him as "Tonto," and the car drives away with him in it. We hear the phrase "We are brothers," and in the film, another scenario is visualized wherein the mounted policeman, himself a Native American, deals differently with his disturbed Native "brother." The policeman is shown walking the horse with the young man in handcuffs on it, leading them away peaceably.

We watch Redroad watch the city go by while lying against a tree in Central Park. His view is of a Trojan horse sculpture that is juxtaposed with the Manhattan skyline as one of the city's tourist attractions; a horse-drawn carriage passes by. Riding in one of the carriages is the white couple who arrived earlier that morning on the tourist boat.

The film cuts to a scene underneath an elevated highway, which may be FDR Drive alongside the East River. We see that the fish stolen earlier

Still from *High Horse*. Photograph courtesy of director Randy Redroad.

has been cooked and eaten; only its skeleton remains as the African-American sits by the small fire he built to cook the fish. The elder Native American walks up and looks down at the fire. The young man gestures for the older man to sit down and offers him a banana. He accepts it and begins eating it with a smile on his face. No words are exchanged. The young man answers his cell phone, gets up to leave, and shakes the elder's hand, leaving the older man staring at the coals as we hear the crackle of the small fire. The older man stretches his arms and legs and picks up the bag of remaining bananas, and the vignette is summarized with a voice-over: "No matter what the weather—the city has its nature."

A cut is made to the drummers in the park. Two officers in a police car stare at them beating their drums. They nod at each other disapprovingly but continue driving through the park. The police officers both have hairy sideburns, which make them look like the criminals, rather than the drummers, who are enjoying themselves.

A transition is made to Redroad riding his bicycle, darting in and out of traffic, making it a sport to weave between the cars, taxis, and buses.

There is a cut to the elder Native, minding his own business, sitting somewhere downtown, and we see the white couple walk up to him. This chance meeting is remotely similar to meeting him on a reservation. The woman bursts out, "My god, that's a picture." Her husband offers the Native man a dollar to take his photograph. The elder puts up two fingers. That settled, the "Indian" begins to stand up for the photo; however, the woman gestures him to remain seated. He smiles and is told, "Don't smile." After taking the photo, they hand the elder one dollar bill torn into two pieces, and hurriedly leave. But the encounter is not over. The woman gets into their recreational vehicle as the husband begins to follow her, but the Native man grabs him from behind and throws him to the ground. He gets into the vehicle instead; after a slight delay, the wife screams. The elder throws her out of the RV as well, then he gets out of the vehicle and gives the couple a necklace made from paper clips. He gets back into the RV, and as he closes the door, we can see "1492" on the door. The elder drives away, leaving the couple stunned and lying on the street, staring at the welcome mat that is on fire.

The African-American bicycle messenger shares a moment in the park with the drummers. Redroad is seen locking his bicycle to a basement stair railing at an apartment building. Although we do not see the bicycle being taken, a quick cut in the film shows that it was stolen. Afterward, Redroad walks away looking as though he's lost his best friend. We see him walk aimlessly, and then he has what is the equivalent of a spiritual awakening. An apartment building, from Redroad's point of view, becomes illuminated with white light, and a flock of birds fly over the building. The moment passes quickly in the film, and Redroad wanders into an empty lot with piles of rubbish and other discarded building materials. He sits and lowers his head.

The film and the day are coming to a close. The African-American couple are reunited as they return to their apartment building at the same time. Redroad is seen lying in the park, and a mounted policeman calls out to him, "Sleeping Beauty, if you want to sleep go to a shelter," assuming that Redroad is homeless. After the officer gets no response from Redroad, he dismounts and walks over and kicks Redroad's shoe, which stirs him. Redroad rises and walks away, but stops suddenly, turns and leaps on the horse, and gallops away. The officer pulls out his gun and aims it at Redroad. The Native elder appears as a spirit and says to the officer, "You already sent a brother to jail today. Are you going to send another to his grave?" and disappears. The officer drops his arm with the gun to his side and recalls the image of the younger Native man he had arrested earlier. The officer's eyes shut tightly as he raises his arms toward the sky. At about the same time, the horse returns to him free of the saddle and reins.

The film does not end there.

The Native woman who spent her day fishing at the park pond hears flute music, and we watch her search for the music's origin. Meanwhile, her partner in the business suit is looking for her in the park. She is consumed by the flute playing and eventually finds Redroad playing his flute in a tent and smiles approvingly. The Native elder is seen standing nearby, and he, too, smiles broadly. The film cuts to black with the words "High Horse."

The film ends as it opens, the start of another story. Redroad's film reminds me of "High Horse's Courting," as told by Nick Black Elk in *Black Elk Speaks,* written by John Niehardt. It is Black Elk's story of a courtship in their camp by a young man named High Horse who tried several times, unsuccessfully, to earn the approval of the parents of a young woman with whom he was in love. Black Elk recalls that High Horse was so lovesick that he didn't care what happened, and made a real fool of himself by trying to steal the woman instead of proving his worthiness as a provider. Ultimately, High Horse did win the proper approval after stealing a herd of enemy horses and running them through the camp, which led to his getting the girl.[12] Redroad's flute playing in the park brings a kindred spirit to him in the form of a Native woman, which happens after he has given into or surrendered to the forces of the city.

The Native woman's fishing in the park pond while her male partner goes off to work in a business suit suggests that she has a lot of free time, does not need to work, or is temporarily out of work. Longing and boredom are apparent in her posture, but upon hearing the flute, she perks up and runs to find its origin. As she approaches Redroad playing his flute, she is already in love. It is no coincidence that certain Native communities refer to some flute playing as love-flute music.

There have been many Native American women who came to live and work in New York City. Maria Tallchief (Osage) from Oklahoma became America's prima ballerina with the New York City Ballet, and was married to its director George Balanchine. Today many young Native American women come to New York to pursue acting careers, including Irene Bedard, who is the Native woman in Redroad's film.

Redroad makes maximum use of ignorance in his use of caricature, illustrated by the white couple whose stereotypes of Indians are typical. When the Native elder takes the couple's RV in exchange for a paper-clip necklace, it is clearly a comment about the cultural myth associated with Manhattan. Taking the RV in exchange for beads or taking the land in exchange for beads, in this context, represents the same transaction of theft. Redroad's commentary with regard to his own Native perspective concerning freedom is revealed when he steals the police horse and returns it without reins. The cultural perception of freedom projected in the film by Redroad is akin to letting go of the need to be in control and dominating other people, places, and animals.

▶

Hands of History (1994), Dir. Loretta Todd, National Film Board of Canada

Hands of History (1994) is a film directed by Loretta Todd (Métis/Cree) and is a production of the National Film Board of Canada, Studio D, a studio within the Film Board that produces films by and about women.[13] Todd's film features the carving tradition and textile artistry of Doreen Jensen from Hazelton, the basket weaving tradition preserved by Rena Point Bolton from the Frazier Valley, painting and installation by Joane Cardinal Schubert from Calgary, and multiple media paintings by Jane Ash Poitras from Edmonton.

Todd reveals the individual personalities of each artist in profiles that revolve around a narrative presented in a keynote presentation by Doreen Jensen at a gathering to honor her contributions to Aboriginal art. Jensen's speech addresses the misinterpretation of Aboriginal art and culture by Euro-Canadian historians, who have imposed their biases in the interpretation of Aboriginal art. The film, however, is not overtly political, nor does it position the featured women as representing all Aboriginal artists.

A "Women's Honor Song" begins in black that dissolves into an extreme close-up of a beaded pattern superimposed on "The National Film Board of Canada, Studio D Production." A close-up of dentalium shells transitions to a floral design made of porcupine quills. These motifs establish that Doreen Jensen is speaking about art as we hear her say, "In my language, there is no word for art. This is not because we are devoid of art; art is so powerfully integrated with all aspects of life, we are replete with it." Todd incorporates archival film footage of Aboriginal women in Native dress walking in file formation as Jensen continues, "As Aboriginal artists, we need to reclaim our work, our heritage, and our future." The film title *Hands of History* is superimposed on another archival photo of Aboriginal women looking camera-shy.

The first artist profiled is Doreen Jensen (Gitksan), who shares her childhood memory of playing by the river where "those totem poles tell our family histories." As she looks up at the eagle carved on the pole, it also appears to look down at her. Jensen continues to talk about her interest in carving, masks, and totems, and she shares anecdotes about the excitement she felt when she began; while working in her living room, on her good furniture, she was not able to sleep because she wanted to keep going.

A jazz trumpet solo plays as still photographs of Rena Point Bolton (Salish)[14] show her weaving a basket as a young woman. Close-ups of her fingers emphasize their importance as we hear her say, "I was considered a great find in the 1950s or 60s, that I still remembered how to weave bulrush. I was found weaving a basket that I had dug the roots and split myself. . . . To this day I don't think of myself as an artist, I just think of myself as being obedient to the teaching of my elders, and I'm passing my teachings to the next generation." Todd uses the opportunity to show Bolton outdoors with her family collecting bark and roots for her baskets.

The sound of Joane Cardinal Schubert (Métis) painting a large canvas gives way to time-lapse film editing that shows different stages of her painting. Schubert's voice-over says, "It was a discipline [art] that crossed boundaries—and there were clearly boundaries—for Native people when I was going to school."

The film's tempo is changed with Native music, and the voice of Jane Ash Poitras (Cree) is heard as scenes of a cloudy sky grow and fill the sky in various shades of gray: "Some of the first images I remember as a child are mostly from nature. I guess that's what it would be for every child looking at the sky and clouds and the awareness, the way they would move, you see animals and people, and you'd see a whole movie."

The introduction of the women functions as a palette for Todd throughout the rest of the film. At this point in the film, however, Todd interposes a separate narrative: a white male researcher in a lab coat walks into a simple stage set and seats himself at a desk surrounded by artifacts. As the man picks up a mask, Doreen Jensen's voice-over is heard: "The first Europeans called our art primitive and vulgar. Today . . . craft and artifact. The single worst thing that happened was that academics tended to freeze our art into certain time periods. We need to communicate in our own words, our own voices, what it is that we're doing."

Jensen is interviewed in her home; she stands next to a shelf with an unpainted carved mask strongly resembling her own facial character lines. She continues, "Because up until now our work has been defined by outsiders, and it's difficult for an outsider to define the art that I'm making or that other people are making unless they're part of that." Archival film footage depicts Aboriginal women with baskets tied to their backs who are seen at a riverbed using long-handled digging sticks; a separate film clip shows other women picking berries. A slow-motion clip of a basket being woven is a transition to Rena Point Bolton.

Bolton is seen with several baskets before her on a table as she shares information about the utility of baskets: "The baskets were used for cooking, carrying water, picking berries. . . . open-weave baskets were for washing fish heads, washing clams, for washing seaweed. Cedar bark for ceremonies—you stand on the mat to receive your name—it was an honor to stand on the mat of an elder who wove this with her hands." Bolton refers to ancestral canoe carvers and weavers, who were special people in the community and highly respected, as an archival photograph shows an Aboriginal woman surrounded by hundreds of baskets.

Jensen and Bolton are both advocates and educators who have used their art to question the systematic dismissal of Aboriginal people and culture. According to Jensen, "everywhere I looked, books, museums, our artifacts were there, but our voice was never there." She began working with a committee to establish a museum in Hazelton in the 1960s, recalling what an elder said to her: "You can't call it a museum, museums are places where you keep objects of a dead culture. Our culture is not dead, it's only sleeping." Jensen heard that as a reason to be a part of reawakening Aboriginal culture and went on to become an artist and curator.

Bolton refers to herself in the film as a rebel. She tells about how she made a political stand against the Canadian government, which had outlawed potlatch ceremonies in the 1920s. She says that to prove to her community that potlatching was not wrong, she held her own potlatch and made cedar-bark skirts and capes for her children. Photographs of her children in their ceremonial regalia, which she wove herself, are beautiful and capture the spirit of Bolton's rebellion. Bolton's potlatch ceremony is a remarkable demonstration of the courage of Aboriginal women who have taken political stands against prejudicial laws that forced a fear of reprisal on Native people both in the United States and Canada. In the film, Bolton is beautifully poised, quietly spoken, and modest. Finally, Bolton's advocacy on behalf of her community is reinforced by her own admission that a belief in spiritual principles proves there is nothing wrong with the way Native people celebrate life.

Joane Cardinal Schubert and Jane Ash Poitras represent the generation succeeding that of Bolton and Jensen. Their personal experiences define their art in relationship to specific circumstances in their lives that inspired them to create. Schubert identifies an encounter with another Aboriginal student while attending art school that motivated her to study her own family heritage. Poitras's childhood experience, however, was radically altered after her mother's death. She was removed from the community and grew up in an urban setting without the benefit of family that cared about her.

Schubert and Poitras use their formal art training to explore Euro-Canadian government policies for Aboriginal peoples, which continue to have an impact because they still are not resolved. Schubert illustrates the perception of First Nations people through multimedia installations that require audience participation in self-reflexive exercises about Native history or that reposition the viewer's physical position for viewing her art and message. Poitras has refined her mixed-media collage paintings that are stories in themselves. Among her painting narratives is "Oka," referring to the confrontation that took place in Quebec Province in 1990. At issue were Mohawks who sought to prevent the expansion of a golf course over ancestral burials, and the militia response by the provincial and federal governments of Canada that led to a seventy-eight day standoff.

We feel the film coming to closure with the conclusion of Jensen's address: "Canada is an image that hasn't emerged yet." Her commentary about Aboriginal art weaves throughout the film. She says, "Because this country hasn't recognized its First Nations, its whole foundation is shaking." A basket by Bolton and a painting by Schubert are intercut with Jensen saying, "If Canada is to emerge as a nation with a cultural identity and purpose, we have to accept First Nations art." As a mask carving by Jensen is projected, she continues, ". . . about what it has to tell us about the spirit and the land. If you really pay attention, you can get the message without diminishing it or appropriating it." Audience applause concludes the film, which is dedicated to the featured artists and "all Aboriginal women artists."

The final scene in the film is of Rena Point Bolton walking with her grandchildren on a typically cloudy day in the Northwest. As they walk by two men carving a canoe, the film frame freezes on Bolton's grandson looking up at the camera. Bolton's voice-over says, "It's quite a job raising ten children; everything I know has to be carried on, and if no one can carry it, then surely all of them together will be able to carry it on."

Hands of History is a groundbreaking film that conveys the power of stories when the words take hold of a storyteller and "go their own way and become the language of experience, sensation, history, and imagination."[15] The historical perspective regarding art and its significant influence in Native communities is applicable not only to Aboriginal art in Canada but also to Native art in the United States. Alfred Young Man (Cree), artist and art professor, commented in 1988 at a National Native Indian Artists' Symposium for artists from the United States and Canada that "the borders may divide us physically but they don't spiritually." The representation of Native women and the acknowledgment made by Todd of Aboriginal women actually preserving the art tradition and cultural practices is illuminating. Todd's selective use of archival photographs and film footage connects the past differently to the present by establishing the survival of cultural traditions rather than their demise.

Finally, *Hands of History* positions art made by Aboriginal women in a political context. The film empowers Native women to examine, in their own words, their intellectual and political space as leaders of their communities as well as in the larger context of art production. Georges E. Sioui, a Canadian historian of Huron ancestry, proposed a concept of "Amerindian autohistory" as a method for documenting Aboriginal cultures. He argues that Aboriginal oral tradition leads to historical insights in comprehending the original culture. Sioui writes, "Such a method would be a basis for establishing a new history to match the image of themselves that people have always had, or should have."[16] As depicted in Todd's film, using art as an act of resistance is understood differently by Aboriginal people when viewed as protecting and preserving cultural heritage, as illustrated by Bolton's potlatch. Todd's filmic skill demonstrates Sioui's methodology of autohistory and captures the central role that Aboriginal women have always had in their communities of origin and in determining the survival of their people.

▶━━

A Video Book (1994), Dir. Beverly R. Singer

Early in 1994, my grandmother Florence Singer showed me a photograph taken in the 1930s of her mother, father, and brother, my great-grandparents and great uncle. I asked her permission, which she granted me, to reproduce the photograph in my work. The archival photograph was tinted and the photographer had painted a Plains feathered bonnet on my great uncle's head. Photography is a strong interest of mine that began in childhood, inspired by my grandfather Lawrence Singer, since deceased, who owned a Brownie camera. One particular photograph, taken by my Grandpa Lawrence, is of me about the age of six and my Aunt Amy, who was about eleven years old in 1960. We are both all smiles and dressed in Navajo-styled velvet blouses and skirts, lavished in silver and turquoise bracelets, necklaces, and concho belts. The heads-only portrait photograph of my great-grandparents taken by a white photographer was a beginning for me to tell my own story.

In 1994, after many life trials, including facing my own alcohol abuse, I produced *A Video Book,* which embodies my healing resurgence at the time. During my visit home to Santa Clara Pueblo, when my grandmother loaned me the photograph, I made a presentation about my work to the third-grade class at the Santa Clara Pueblo Day School. They sang a song to me they had composed, "Each Kid Is Special." I had just received the cassette, and I knew it was meant for this project. I called and asked Keith Secola if I could use a beautiful guitar solo he wrote titled "Wassnondae." I went to a friend's video editing studio in Los Angeles at ten o'clock in the morning with a cartridge of slides and began talking at the images. I completed editing the video at six o'clock that same day.

■───────────────────────────────────────

Narration from A Video Book

(A photograph of my fingers preparing to open a book) The power that is in the land, the sky, and the air we breathe comes from knowing that ancestors who prepared the way for us who are alive today left us with a beautiful legacy. (Photographs of the sky and earth shapes and Mesa Verde Anasazi dwellings)

When I see pictures of ugly Indians or stupid Indians or sad Indians I know they are not me. (Cross-eyed Indian wearing a phony headband and feather)

Because I know when I was stupid and sad and ugly was when I was drinking alcohol. (Photo of me eating with a bottle of beer before me)

I'd forgotten the beauty of our old dances, the deer dances—their power, their beauty. (Deer dancers at San Juan Pueblo)

I'd forgotten that I live in a modern world that is filled with things of long ago and things from today that take me away. (My mother's Pueblo oven superimposed on a cafeteria kitchen)

I layer the images of my great-grandparents and my great uncle. All who have gone on to the spirit world, and I place them in the Grand Canyon for safe keeping. (The Grand Canyon is superimposed over archival photograph of my great-grandparents)

I look at myself and I do see a slice of the past. *(Photo of myself superimposed over a 1950s car)*

I grew up in a little town called Espanola, located in northern New Mexico, and I remember when Willie's Pool Hall was open and the Arrow Motel still received guests. *(Flickering lights surround a photograph of Willie's Pool Hall and the Arrow Motel with a sign in front of it of an Indian shooting a bow and arrow)*

I look around my office walls today, and on my shelves I see an altar, and on the altar are horses, a picture of Frida Kahlo,[17] sage, rocks. I like collecting rocks. *(Objects shown on my office shelf)*

I look at the same activities that the church conducts each year as they baptize and christen and celebrate the first Holy Communions. The children look like little angels. *(Image of boys and girls from my Pueblo outside the Santa Clara Catholic Church dressed in white for First Communion)*

But angels are mystical and magical and these children, too, can be that. *(Computer replicates the photo of the children into twenty-five smaller cells)*

As I said, I like the ideas presented in Frida Kahlo's work. But I didn't say that before, so I have to start over [laughter]. I just like the ideas presented in Frida Kahlo's work. *(Frida Kahlo replicated into twenty-five smaller cells, creating a pattern)*

When the trains came and the highways were built and the field processing plants were constructed, everything happened so fast. *(Image of an Amtrak train dissolves to a fuel plant with smoke that fills the screen with black)*

There are some films that were made by Navajos that were documented in a book called *Through Navajo Eyes*; it was a special project in the sixties. If you ever get a chance try and see some of those old films they produced. They sit in the collection at the Museum of Modern Art in New York. *(Book cover showing a Navajo woman in traditional dress holding a film camera)*

I turn the pages on my life, *(the computer turns the previous image like a page)* and I look out over the landscape, and I see our sacred mountain. It fills me with a lot of strength and courage. *(Image of snow-covered ground and a mountain in the distance)*

The old drive-in theaters that my sisters and I used to go to with our parents were a lot of fun. *(Photo of the Espanola Starlighter Drive-In, just before it was demolished in 1994)*

But I don't remember seeing *Nanook of the North*. *(An image of Nanook in his kayak moves across the screen)* I do remember seeing stagecoach images with the arrival of the outsiders, that's when things changed. *(Archival photograph of a wagon train with flashing words on the screen reads "SALE 50% OFF")*

I hope we've seen the "Last of the Mohicans" films. *(Several rapid images show a photo from the 1920s film of a Mohican with a knife at the throat of a settler)*

My great-grandpa and my great-uncle. They say I sat on the lap of my great-grandfather. That makes me feel good, because his energy runs through me today. *(Photograph of my great-grandfather and great-uncle taken around 1930)*

And for all the Native American people across the United States, these dots show us that we are everywhere, still. *(U.S. map with black dots)*

We're shooting back with cameras these days, and, yes, we are making our own films and videos, and I, too, am a filmmaker. *(Blurred image of young Native male jumping at the camera)*

I did a lot of things in my life, some good, some not so good. *(Image of my résumé)*

But the fact is that today is a new day, and I live my life with a lot of thanks for each day the Creator has given me. *(Ceremonial hands drag off the screen as it changes color from deep red to green)*

Kunda.

My personal story is an invitation for others to examine what is meaningful in their lives. Art curator Theresa Harlan (Laguna/Santo Domingo/Jemez Pueblo) writes that "As Native people, we must claim right to, and ownership of, strategic and intellectual space for our works."[18] She also emphasizes the need for Natives to recognize that photos and other images have been used to usurp Native people's own history in an attempt to categorize our experience to fit the needs of a commercial society. *A Video Book* invokes an honesty that has been the bedrock upon which I find acceptance of who I am.

Older Native American storytelling traditions are not practiced as they were in the past. Where once community members gathered together at specific times and places to share stories after all the chores were done or after a celebration before retiring in the evening, they now watch videos, which should not be mistaken for Native productions.

The stories I heard in my youth ranged from humorous Coyote exploits to memories shared by my grandmother and her sisters about their time at boarding school. In the stories, Coyote was always making a fool of himself by trying to get food from other animals, like a skunk, through trickery. I remember those times in the late 1960s with my cousins in the mountains as we listened to our aunt tell us stories that brought us closer together. We lacked nothing and felt safe and happy. It's been a long time since I sat and listened to older stories being shared among relatives, largely due to the fact that I am separated from my family by distance. They still tell stories, but the older stories are seldom told.

The kind of stories that we are telling in films are different from the kind of stories that I think of as traditional or ancestral ones. Native film-makers are searching for ways to recollect our memories so that we can restore the feelings of safety and happiness that I experienced in my youth. When I watch a Native-produced film or video, I strongly identify with stories that reconnect me with the Native community, particularly those that demonstrate a struggle to rescue and protect cultural knowledge and history.

I decided to discuss the productions of Victor Masayesva Jr., Sandra Osawa, Arlene Bowman, Randy Redroad, Loretta Todd, and my own because they personalize our lives in this century inasmuch as they also demonstrate the spirit of the older storytelling practices. I watched Masayesva's first produc-tion and recognized a continuance of a way of life that did not have to be explained to me, though that may not be the case for non-Hopi, but that is why his work represents a demonstration of individuality in his use of film. American Indian cultural sovereignty, as represented in the film by Sandra Osawa, provides the ugly portrait of racism in the United States that con-tinues to be experienced by Native people. The irony of having legally sanctioned Aboriginal title to land and rights to hunt and fish often further engage Euro-American radicals who pridefully act out their historically rooted antipathy for Indians in front of cameras. Arlene Bowman's search for self-acceptance as a Navajo and her desire to reconnect with her rela-tives after a long separation may be seen as reasons for *not* using film to reestablish personal family relations. Randy Redroad's fiction film has many elements of older storytelling: he revisits situations and allows his characters to follow through with actions that are personally self-redeeming. It is my belief that Native women perform the bulk of the responsibility and work in maintaining Native practices. Loretta Todd's film presents that truth in film about Aboriginal women artists and culture carriers. My production characterizes my thoughts, feelings, and ideas about being and becoming culturally stronger after a period of alcohol abuse that was rela-tive to the importance I had placed on mainstream American values instead of on my cultural foundation as belonging to a community where I would always have a place to call home, Kapogeh (also known as Santa Clara Pueblo). It has been my experience, and that of many others as well, to make a conscious decision to realign ourselves with our ancestral lifeline and to use it to live a healthier modern cultural life. The value of our film-making efforts today are in direct relationship to Native storytelling prac-tices that are born from memory and encourage us to live as right-sized citizens—meaning seeing oneself as no less and no more than any other human being, but on an equal stature with all people—in the world.

Conclusion
Continuing the Legacy

In his keynote address at the 1991 Two Rivers Native American Film and Video Festival, Roger Buffalohead (Ponca) discussed the shared responsibility that Native Americans have to keep their culture alive: "We are carriers of a rich tribal tradition, and our ancestors left us with a rich legacy that we are now responsible for." While Native American filmmakers continue to work with non-Native institutions and individuals—such as the Center for Media, Culture, and History at New York University and the Smithsonian National Museum of the American Indian—we also have begun to take even more responsibility for the rich cultural legacy Buffalohead refers to by creating our own alliances, festivals, and other means of support for the development, funding, and distribution of our films.

Native Americans have begun to take over the business end of film and media production, thus lessening our reliance on grants and other institutional support from outside of our communities. We have witnessed the emergence of Native American business ventures that have financed films like *Naturally Native* (1997) by Valerie Red Horse (Cherokee/Sioux) and her partner Jennifer Wynne Farmer, who were funded by the Mashantucket Pequot Tribal Nation with its casino profits. In 1998, screenings of the film were held in Los Angeles and at numerous film festivals, but a national theatrical release did not happen.

The Kickapoo Indian Tribe of Kansas has made advances in this area by starting an Outlaw Music Channel, a satellite network dedicated to American Indian heritage and vintage country music.[1] The United Native American Television Broadcasting Council was another group of individuals attempting to organize through the Internet, but it was unsuccessful in starting a Native and Aboriginal broadcasting network in the United States.[2]

During the past twenty years, the greatest advances in Native broadcast media have occurred in Canada. The reason for this rests with the foresight of Aboriginal organizations who collaborated with Aboriginal communities in negotiations over Aboriginal rights with the Canadian government and pressed for greater access to the media. More than twenty years have passed since the federal government in Canada initiated the Anik satellite projects among Aboriginal people in the North, whose isolation became the inspiration for the creation of an Aboriginal television network.

On September 1, 1999, the Aboriginal Peoples Television Network (APTN) became Canada's newest national television network. Representing a milestone for Aboriginal people in Canada, it is the first time in broadcast history that indigenous stories will be produced for international audiences and broadcast on a national television network dedicated to Aboriginal programming. The APTN has its broadcast headquarters in Winnipeg and corporate offices in Ottawa. The programming consists of Aboriginal-produced documentaries, news magazines, drama, entertainment specials, children's series, cooking shows, and other education programs. More than 90 percent of the APTN's programming originates in Canada and is broadcast in English, French, and a number of Aboriginal languages.

First Americans in the Arts is a not-for-profit trust organization comprised of Native and non-Native professionals from the entertainment industry. The organization sponsors the annual First Americans in the Arts Awards in Hollywood to recognize Native actors and supporters of Native people in the entertainment industry.[3] Their sixth awards program in 1998 was a memorable night, where Native people celebrated their film and television stars by mimicking the Oscars. National Aboriginal Achievement Awards are sponsored in Canada, and in March 1998 the program was broadcast by the Canadian Broadcasting Corporation.

The production of episodic television started with *The Rez*. The series, produced by the Canadian Broadcasting Corporation, features an Aboriginal cast and music that is set in a community named Kidabinessee.[4] A newer popular televised series, *North of 60,* is coproduced by Alliance Communications Corporation and Alberta Filmworks, Inc., non-Aboriginal companies who received support from the Canadian Broadcasting Corporation to produce the series. The series is about a small northern town named Lynx River with a population of 150 that *looks in* at the problems and lives of an Aboriginal community. It features a Native cast, and one of the cowriters is Aboriginal but is not named.

Native American films and videos that contribute to a truer conception of Native people are still not widely available to the public. In order to reach a broader audience, we need better distribution for our works. If the public knew these films existed, it is more likely that distributors, television programmers, film executives, media management companies, journalism editors, corporate sponsors, cable TV network owners, and public policy makers could be persuaded to support Native-produced work. Ultimately, change will only come about when, as Yvonne Beamer, director of Nichen/ Family Awareness Network, points out, people "get used to seeing our way and respecting our way."[5]

► ──

Festivals and Alliances

Film festivals are an important means for filmmakers in emerging or non-mainstream areas to get their films screened and recognized. For example, the initiatives for Native cinema sponsored by the Sundance Institute and Sundance Festival have been significant. In 1994, the Sundance Festival began a Native American program category. By allowing video into the film-only focus of the festival, Native Americans were able to participate where otherwise our absence might have gone on indefinitely. It is significant that the Sundance Institute, whose endorsement of film projects by American Indians, including *Grand Avenue,* for HBO, and *Smoke Signals,* has made it possible for them to reach national audiences, was founded by Robert Redford, a Hollywood insider.

We have also started organizing our own film festivals. In 1975, the first American Indian Film Festival was held in Seattle and has since been held annually in San Francisco. Michael Smith (Choctaw) founded the festival and later began the American Indian Film Institute (AIFI). The AIFI, in addition to sponsoring the festival, began publishing *ICE,* a magazine that included interviews with Native American actors and highlights about Native productions.

In 1982, Ted Jojola (Isleta), professor of architecture at the University of New Mexico, organized "The American Indian Image on Film: The Southwest," the first major film festival at a university campus to address the topic of Indian movie images.[6] In addition to the film screenings, a dialogue was initiated among festival participants regarding Hollywood, stereotypes, and Native filmmaking. Jojola was assisted by actor and storyteller Geraldine Keams (Navajo), who was instrumental in getting Hollywood participation at the festival, including a presentation by Robert Redford. Other presentations at the festival were given by numerous writers and scholars, including Gretchen Bataille, writers Ralph and Natasha Friar, writer Simon Ortiz;[7] and Native filmmakers Lena Carr, Bob Hicks, Larry Littlebird, and Phil Lucas, who were joined by Elizabeth Weatherford and Emelia Seubert, representing the Film and Video Program of the Heye Foundation, Museum of the American Indian.

Harry Fonseca, "American Indian Image on Film: The Southwest," for the Native American Studies Center, University of New Mexico, 1982. Image courtesy of Ted Jojola.

Native American films and videos have increased representation internationally at film festivals in Austria, Ecuador, France, Germany, Japan, Mexico, and Spain. The Native-sponsored Dreamspeakers Festival in Edmonton, Canada, and Two Rivers Native American Film and Video Festival in Minneapolis were both founded in 1991. These festivals provide a base of support for our filmmaking, and they encourage new filmmakers to begin the process. Native Arts Circle, an advocacy organization for art and artists in Minnesota and sponsor of the Two Rivers Native American Film and Video Festival, embraces the idea of creating a sacred space to honor films and videos produced by Native people:

> The vision was to bring to our community a Native film and video festival that honors the richness of our cultures while celebrating the strength of the native spirit. As we began to organize we found many creative people who were honoring this spirit. We spoke with them and learned of their work, it became apparent that the messages and stories they were telling were ones that all people need to hear. Their stories reveal the endurance of our cultures and our connections to our earth mother. . . . these new storytellers and visionaries of our people . . . are using their gifts to describe in our own words and images who we are as Native people. They are helping us to reclaim our identities while challenging others to rethink their perceptions of us.[8]

Founded in 1983 by American Indians, the American Indian Registry for the Performing Arts was an advocacy organization that focused on helping tribally enrolled Native Americans secure employment in motion pictures and television in Hollywood. A founding member of the Registry was actor Will Sampson, who was instrumental in organizing an advisory committee that included Hollywood actors Burt Reynolds, Claude Akins, Hoyt Axton, Ralph Bellamy, Max Gail, Dennis Weaver, and Jonathan Winters. The Registry produced *The American Indian Talent Directory,* which went to motion picture, television, and other performing arts producers. Registry members received *The Entertainment Industry Guide,* a monthly newsletter, as well as opportunities to attend film and TV industry seminars, acting workshops, and casting assistance. In 1994, beset by a lack of financial support, the registry ceased operation. Many Native American actors who achieved prominence in the nineties, including Wes Studi and Tantoo Cardinal, had been members of the registry.

The history and development of media by Native people demonstrates a highly independent spirit of production efforts, but Aboriginal and Native American filmmakers have at times found it necessary to build alliances as a way to challenge the mainstream inequities in funding Native projects. In 1991, an Aboriginal Film and Video Alliance was discussed among filmmakers who attended the International Indigenous Film Festival in Japan. The Alliance was officially established in August 1993, in partnership with the Banff Centre for the Arts in Edmonton. The Banff Centre offered its facility as a gathering place for Aboriginal artists. The Alliance provided a statement of purpose that read: "To govern ourselves means to govern our stories. . . . To re-imagine and reclaim our ground in the intimate, small, everyday things of life and community is to become self-governing."[9]

Another alliance, the Native American Producers Alliance (NAPA), was organized at the 1993 Two Rivers Native American Film and Video Festival in Minneapolis. NAPA was organized in response to the continuation of white productions about Indians in which opportunities for Indians to work in key production roles were impossible to attain. More than just an advocacy group, NAPA was a political voice committed to the issue of tribal membership as a key criteria for membership to the Alliance. It also raised questions about tribal ownership of culture and stories and promoted dialogue about aesthetics and tribal sovereignty.

In 1993, the Native American Producers Alliance sponsored the Imagining Indians: Native American Film and Video Festival in Scottsdale, Arizona. Victor Masayesva Jr. served as the festival's artistic director and retained cosponsorship of the festival from the Scottsdale Center for the Arts and Atlatl. Atlatl's support was important because it is a nationally recognized American Indian organization whose purpose is to heighten awareness of indigenous aesthetics and expression. Margaret Wood, chair of Atlatl's First Circle board of directors, pronounced the festival a landmark event exploring media representation of indigenous peoples from our own perspective. Atlatl's participation in the festival was an opportunity to address a new constituency of artists—Native American film and video makers.[10] One of the panel discussions was an invitation to tribal representatives in the Southwest to discuss their views regarding intellectual property rights and the appropriation of Native cultures in media. The panel was moderated by Masayesva and included Herman Agoyo (Tewa), former governnor of San Juan Pueblo; Delmar Boni (San Carlos Apache), indigenous healer; Leigh Jenkins (Hopi), curator and cultural preservationist; Kathy Sanchez (Tewa), educator and filmmaker from San Ildefonso Pueblo; and Merata Mita (Maori), filmmaker from New Zealand. The comments by Merata Mita summarized the conclusions reached by the panel: "Each of us has a language, an identity, and a culture that belong nowhere else in the world except where we come from, and that's who we are. Where we live, where we come from, defines us. We determine who we gift, because when we gift any part of our culture, we're gifting part of ourselves."[11]

While they may not be significant in the larger context of mainstream dialogue, my point in repeating these affirmations by indigenous people is that as filmmakers we need to support each other and in turn feel ourselves supported. We draw energy at these meetings and return home ready to work on new productions, but that is just one part of our lives. Most of us are members of communities where we have responsibilities as parents, employees, leaders, students, or any combination thereof.

Culture informs who we are and who we are becoming. It guides our filming, televising, dramatizing, music, writing, cartooning, and photography. Newer filmmaking projects have potential commercial opportunities that earlier films and videos did not. In the brief history that is outlined, many more stories are patiently waiting to be told. My faith in Native American filmmaking is that it will continue to raise the consciousness in our society toward a healthy, informed understanding of our history and cultures presently and for those coming after us.

▶

Epilogue

Wiping the war paint off the lens is an imaginary scenario from the time I found a colossal old movie camera that was used to film those wild Indian battles in the early days of Hollywood. I looked through the dusty lens and saw splattered spots that turned out to be old, crusted face paint, part of the makeup that had been used for phony war paint. I used my T-shirt to wipe off the lens, and that started me thinking about films that showed Indians differently. I wondered if a toxic solvent would clean the lens. The absurdity of the situation brings me to a moment of clarity that

Darren Robes Kipp, line producer, wiping the lens during filming of *Backbone of the World: The Blackfeet* (1997), director George Burdeau; Laura Thomas, photographer. Courtesy of Rattlesnake Productions, Inc.

reminds me it is good to dream, but it must be followed by hard work to bring the dream to reality.

When the song and dance are finished, we take our evergreens to the creek, returning them to the earth. They are a symbol and spirit of the eternal life that we dance to affirm by giving thanks to everything. Kunda.

Notes

Foreword

1. Paul Chaat Smith, "Land of a Thousand Dances," in *Exile on Main Street*, http://redplanet.home. mindspring.com.

Prologue

1. Mateo Aragon quoted by Joe S. Sando, *The Pueblo Indians* (San Francisco: Indian Historian, 1976), 163.

Introduction

1. James Axtell, "Colonial America without the Indians: A Counterfactual Scenario," in *Indians in American History*, ed. Frederick E. Hoxie (Arlington Heights, Ill.: Harlan Davidson, 1988), 47.
2. "Métis" is the name used in Canada for mixed blood offspring who trace their roots to fur trappers who married Native women. Métis is an important distinction within Aboriginal communities (Hoxie, *Indians in American History*, 208).
3. D'Arcy McNickle, *Native American Tribalism: Indian Survivals and Renewals* (London: Oxford University Press, 1973), 88.
4. Paula Gunn Allen, *The Sacred Hoop: Recovering the Feminine in American Indian Traditions* (Boston: Beacon Press, 1986), 225.
5. Leslie Marmon Silko, "Language and Literature from a Pueblo Perspective," in *English Literature: Opening Up the Canon*, ed. Leslie Fiedler and Houston A. Baker Jr. (Baltimore: Johns Hopkins University Press, 1981), 57.
6. Simon Ortiz, *After and Before the Lightning* (Tucson: University of Arizona Press, 1994), 20.
7. Paula Gunn Allen, *The Sacred Hoop*, 224.
8. Paula Gunn Allen, *Grandmothers of the Light: A Medicine Woman's Sourcebook* (Boston: Beacon, 1991), 3.
9. Joseph Bruchac, "The Unbroken Circle: Contemporary Iroquois Storytelling," *Northeast Indian Quarterly* 7, no. 4 (winter 1990): 14.
10. Luci Tapahonso, "Singing in Navajo, Writing in English: The Poetics of Four Navajo Writers," *Culturefront* 2, no. 2 (summer 1993): 36–75.
11. Fred Nahwoosky, "Continuity and Change in Native Arts," *Akwe:kon Journal* 11, no. 3/4 (fall/winter 1994): 88.

1. Bringing Home Film and Video Making

1. While enrolled at the University of Illinois, Charlene Teters compiled a collection of correspondence, statements, news articles, and editorials concerning the mascot controversy at the University of Illinois. See her "Indian Identity: Pulled by Different Worlds," *Indian Artist* 4, no. 2 (spring 1998): 12. See also the award-winning documentary *In Whose Honor?* (1996) by Jay Rosenstein, distributed by New Day Films.
2. *In Whose Honor?* by Jay Rosenstein.

3. Artist statement by Charlene Teters, "Dispelling the Myths: Controlling the Image," curated by Joanna Osburn-Bigfeather for the American Indian Community House Gallery, New York (June 3 to September 15, 1993).

4. *Imagining Indians* (1992), Victor Masayesva Jr., 84 min., IS Productions (P.O. Box 747, Hotevilla, AZ 86030).

5. Vine Deloria Jr., *Metaphysics of Modern Existence* (New York: Macmillan, 1978), xi.

6. Bob Jones, "The Seneca's Search for the Past," *Destination Discovery* 9, no. 2 (May 1993): 20.

7. Vine Deloria Jr., *Custer Died for Your Sins* (New York: Avon, 1970), 270.

8. "Debra Lynn White Plume," in *Cante Ohitika Win (Brave-Hearted Women): Images of Lakota Women from the Pine Ridge Reservation, South Dakota*, Carolyn Reyer (Vermillion: University of South Dakota Press, 1991), 61.

9. Faye Ginsburg, "Indigenous Media: Faustian Contract or Global Village?" *Cultural Anthropology* 6, no. 6 (February, 1991): 104.

10. Kathryn Shanley, "The Lived Experience: American Indian Literature after Alcatraz," *Akwe:kon Journal* 11, no. 3/4 (fall/winter 1994): 125.

11. Ginsburg, "Indigenous Media," 94.

12. Welcome statement by Victor Masayesva Jr. in the program catalog for the Imagining Indians: Native American Film and Video Festival, Scottsdale Center for the Arts, Phoenix, 1994, 1.

13. Rich Hill, *Creativity Is Our Tradition: Three Decades of Contemporary Indian Art at the Institute of American Indian Art* (Santa Fe, N.M.: Institute of American Indian Art Press, 1992).

14. Arlene Bowman, "Experiences as an Indian Filmmaker," *Visions* (fall 1990): 10.

15. Calvin Carolyn, "Arlene Bowman: Navajo Filmmaker," *News from Indian Country* 11, no. 4 (28 February 1997): 1B.

16. Ruth Denny, "Open Letter to Ted Turner," *Circle: News from a Native Perspective* (Minneapolis) (March 1993): 6.

17. Dianne Brennan, producer; Richard Weise, director; Gerald Vizenor, writer; Film in the Cities, Minneapolis.

2. The War-Painted Years

1. John G. Cawelti, *Adventure, Mystery, and Romance* (Chicago: University of Chicago, 1976), 193.

2. Ralph Friar and Natasha Friar, *The Only Good Indian: The Hollywood Gospel* (New York: Drama Book Specialists, 1972), 59.

3. Ibid.

4. Ibid., 99.

5. Ibid.

6. Kevin Brownlow, *The War, the West, and the Wilderness* (New York: Knopf, 1979), 331.

7. Ibid.

8. Friar and Friar, *The Only Good Indian*, 176.

9. Ibid., 113.

10. Robert Sklar, *Movie-Made America: A Cultural History of American Movies* (New York: Vintage, 1976), 40.

11. Friar and Friar, *The Only Good Indian*, 123.

12. Ibid. During the Depression, movie producers made salary cuts of 50 percent for most studio employees including studio actors, who typically worked for $65 per six-day week. In 1937, the Screen Actors Guild approved salaries of $35 per day for movie stunt workers and $5.50 per day for extras. During the filming of *Powwow Highway (1989)*, I worked two days as an Indian extra and was paid $50.

13. Ernest A. Dench, "The Dangers of Employing Redskins as Movie Actors," in *The Pretend Indians: Images of Native Americans in the Movies*, ed. Gretchen Bataille and Charles Silet (Ames: Iowa State University Press, 1980), 61.

14. Sklar, *Movie-Made America*, 77.

15. "Inuit" is a self-identified name used today in lieu of Eskimo. "Itkivimuit" refers to an Inuit village.

16. Erik Barnouw, *Documentary: A History of the Non-Fiction Film* (London: Oxford University, 1974), 42.

17. Ibid.

18. Bunny McBride, *Molly Spotted Elk: A Penobscot in Paris* (Norman: University of Oklahoma Press, 1995), 124.

19. Michael T. Marsden and Jack Nachbar, "The Indian in the Movies," in *Handbook of North American Indians*, ed. William C. Sturtevant, vol. 4, *History of Indian-White Relations* (Washington, D.C.: Smithsonian Institution, 1988), 611.

20. McBride, *Molly Spotted Elk*, 125.

21. Interview with Charles Sooktis in *Imagining Indians* (1992), Victor Masayesva Jr., 84 min., IS Productions (P.O. Box 747, Hotevilla, AZ 86030).

22. Friar and Friar, *The Only Good Indian*, 248.
23. Ibid., 134.
24. Marsden and Nachbar, "The Indian in the Movies," 611.
25. Ibid.
26. Virgil J. Vogel, *This Country Was Ours: A Documentary History of the American Indian* (New York: Harper & Row, 1972), 317.
27. Angela Aleiss, "A Race Divided: The Indian Westerns of John Ford," *American Indian Culture and Research Journal* 18, no. 4 (1994): 171.
28. Ibid. See also Alison R. Bernstein, *American Indians and World War II: Toward a New Era in Indian Affairs* (Norman: University of Oklahoma Press, 1991); and Vogel, *This Country Was Ours*, 335.
29. Aleiss, "A Race Divided," 172.
30. *Today Is a Good Day* is a recent film about the life of Chief Dan George, directed by Loretta Todd (Métis/Cree), produced by the National Film Board of Canada.
31. Profile of Jay Silverheels in Richard A. Payne's *Rick & Jim's Real Reel Indians* (Fort Collins, Colo.: Blue Sky Graphics, 1994), 18. A film clip about Silverheels's acting career and advocacy on behalf of Indian actors in Hollywood was screened at the awards banquet on February 7, 1998, sponsored by First Americans in the Arts (P.O. Box 17780, Beverly Hills, CA 90209).
32. Profile of Will Sampson in Payne's *Rick & Jim's Real Reel Indians*, 14.

3. Toward Independence

1. Klara B. Kelly, "Federal Indian Land Policy and Economic Development in the United States," in *Economic Development in American Indian Reservations*, Development Series, no. 1, ed. Roxanne Dunbar Ortiz (Albuquerque: Native American Studies, University of New Mexico, 1979), 34.
2. Vine Deloria Jr., *Behind the Trail of Broken Treaties: An Indian Declaration of Independence* (New York: Dell, 1974), 28.
3. Ibid., 43.
4. Wilma Mankiller and Michael Wallis, *Mankiller: A Chief and Her People* (New York: St. Martin's Press, 1993), 166.
5. The philosophical approach to the arts education program was prepared by Lloyd New, director of arts; in Winona Garmhausen, *History of Indian Arts Education in Santa Fe* (Santa Fe, N.M.: Sunstone Press, 1988), 7.
6. "Indian Education: A National Tragedy—A National Challenge," Report of Special Subcommittee on Indian Education (Washington, D.C.: U.S. Government Printing Office, 1969).
7. Duane Champagne, *Native America: Portrait of the Peoples* (Detroit: Visible Ink Press, 1994), 10–17.
8. Garmhausen, *History of Indian Arts Education in Santa Fe*, 95.
9. Ralph T. Coe, "Lost and Found Traditions: Native American Art 1965–1985" exhibition catalog (New York: University of Washington and the American Federation of Arts, 1986), 9.
10. Timothy Egan, "Backlash Growing as Indians Make a Stand for Sovereignty," *New York Times*, 9 March 1998, A16. The bill introduced by Senator Gorton is S. 1691, American Indian Equal Justice Act (introduced in the Senate, 105th Congress, 2nd Session, February 27, 1998).
11. Vine Deloria Jr. and Clifford M. Lytle, *American Indians, American Justice* (Austin: University of Texas, 1983), 17.
12. Arlene B. Hirschfelder and Martha Kreipe de Montano, *The Native American Almanac: A Portrait of Native America Today* (New York: Prentice Hall, 1993), 25–27.
13. Michelene Fixico, "The Road to Middle Class Indian America," in *American Indian Identity: Today's Changing Perspectives*, ed. Clifford E. Trafzer (Sacramento, Calif.: Sierra Oaks, 1986), 30.
14. Mankiller and Wallis, *Mankiller*, 68.
15. Ibid., 161.
16. Adam Fortunate Eagle, *Alcatraz! Alcatraz! The Indian Occupation of 1969–1971* (Berkeley, Calif.: Heyday, 1992), 20.
17. Lewis Meriam, in *The Problem of Indian Administration*, Brookings Institution, Institute for Government Research (1928; reprint New York: Johnson Reprint, 1971), 573–77.
18. Ibid., 88.
19. Simon J. Ortiz, "The Language We Know," in *I Tell You Now: Autobiographical Essays by Native American Writers*, ed. Brian Swann and Arnold Krupat (Lincoln: University of Nebraska, 1987), 190.
20. Quote of Polingaysi Qoyawayma (Elizabeth Q. White) in Vada F. Carlson's *No Turning Back: A Hopi Indian Woman's Struggle to Live in Two Worlds* (Albuquerque: University of New Mexico Press, 1964), 175.
21. D'Arcy McNickle, *Native American Tribalism: Indian Survivals and Renewals* (London: Oxford University Press, 1973), 117.
22. Clair Huffaker, *Nobody Loves a Drunken Indian* (New York: Dell, 1969).

4. Native Filmmakers, Programs, and Institutions

1. Sol Worth and John Adair, *Through Navajo Eyes: An Exploration in Film Communication and Anthropology* (Bloomington: Indiana University, 1972), 11.
2. See Gregory Bateson, "Exchange of Information about Patterns of Human Behavior," in *Information and Storage and Neutral Control*, ed. William Fields and Walter Abbott (Springfield, Ill.: Charles C. Thomas, 1963). See also Margaret Mead, "Anthropology and the Camera," in *The Encyclopedia of Photography*, vol. 1, ed. Willard D. Morgan (New York: Greystone Press, 1963).
3. The collection of Navajo films includes *A Navajo Weaver* by Susie Benally, *Intrepid Shadows* by Al Clah, *Old Antelope Lake* by Mike Anderson, *The Navajo Silversmith* by Johnny Nelson, *The Spirit of the Navajo* by Maxine and Mary Jane Tsosie, and an untitled film by Alta Kahn. The films are in the film collection at the Museum of Modern Art in New York City and are available for public screening by the museum.
4. Worth and Adair, *Through Navajo Eyes*, 229.
5. Bruce Ignacio interview in Beverly R. Singer's "Film and Video Made by Native Americans: A Cultural Examination of Film and Video Production by Native Americans" (Ph.D. diss., University of New Mexico, 1996), 200.
6. Ibid.
7. Flyer produced by and about the Anthropology Film Center in 1983.
8. Telephone conversation with Harriet Skye, April 28, 1995.
9. Sandra Osawa interview in Singer's "Film and Video Made by Native Amercians," 227.
10. Ibid., 228.
11. "The Native American Videotape Archives 1976–77" catalog foreword (Washington, D.C.: Office of the BIA, U.S. Department of the Interior).
12. Frank Blythe, biography sketch from the program flyer for the Two Rivers Native American Film and Video Festival, "Producer's Forum for Native & Independent Filmmakers" (Community Activists and Art Critics, Law School, University of Minnesota, cosponsored by the Center for Arts Criticism, October 10–11, 1991).
13. "Native American Program Grants," Native American Public Broadcasting Consortium grants announcement (P.O. Box 83111, Lincoln, Nebraska), December 12, 1991.
14. See Elizabeth Weatherford, *Native Americans on Film and Video* (New York: Museum of the American Indian/Heye Foundation, 1981), 93.
15. Dan Lomahaftewa was in New York City to exhibit his art at the First Peoples Gallery in New York City, May 11, 1993, when we had a conversation about his involvement with the Ute Tribal Media program.
16. Gary Robinson interview in Singer's "Film and Video Made by Native Americans," 238.
17. "Films about Native Americans by Native Americans" (1991), publicity brochure from Native Voices Public Television Workshop (Daniel Hart, VCB 224, Montana Public TV, Montana State University, Bozeman, MT 59717).
18. Rennard Strickland, "Coyote Goes Hollywood Part II: If Indians Should Stage a White Man's Play," *Native Peoples* 3, no. 1 (fall 1989): 39.
19. Bob Hicks interview in Singer's "Film and Video Made by Native Americans," 195.
20. "Season 8/1995 Call for Entries," P.O.V., Television with a Point of View (220 West 19th Street, 11th Floor, New York, NY 10011).
21. Robert Hagopian and Phil Lucas, coproducers/codirectors, *Images of Indians* (1980, KCTS/9, Seattle): "Part 1: The Great Movie Massacre," "Part 2: Heathen Injuns and the Hollywood Gospel," "Part 3: How Hollywood Wins the West," "Part 4: The Movie Reel Indians," "Part 5: Warpaint and Wigs."
22. George Burdeau quoted in "American Indians Seek More Say in Film, TV," *Los Angeles Times*, 27 March 1991, F4.
23. Telephone interview with Conroy Chino about his role in *Contact*, December 3, 1997.
24. Conroy Chino interview in Singer's "Film and Video Made by Native Americans," 170.
25. Arlene Hirschfelder, "Profile: Hattie Kauffman, Consumer Reporter of CBS This Morning," *Runner: Native Magazine for Communicative Arts* (Toronto) 1, no. 3 (summer 1994): 21. The *Runner* was renamed *Aboriginal Voices*.
26. Ruby Sootkis interview in Singer's "Film and Video Made by Native Americans," 255.
27. JoAnna Osborne-Bigfeather, former curator, American Indian Community House Gallery, New York City, provided exhibition information of Melanie Printup Hope's multimedia installations in 1993.
28. Press release from Third World Newsreel 1995 Film & Video Production Workshop (335 West 38th Street, 5th Floor, New York, NY 10018), October 28, 1994.
29. The Rockefeller Foundation 1995 U.S. Intercultural Film/Video Fellowship winners announcement, New York.

30. Robert J. Surtees, "Canadian Indian Policies," in *Handbook of North American Indians*, ed. William C. Sturtevant, vol. 4, *History of Indian-White Relations* (Washington, D.C.: Smithsonian Institution, 1988), 89.

31. The Rockefeller Foundation 1995 U.S. Intercultural Film/Video Fellowship winners, 220.

32. Ibid., 222.

33. Ibid., 225.

34. Biography of Zacharias Kunuk in *Revions*, a journal published by the Walter Phillips Gallery, Banff Center for the Arts, 1992.

35. Alanis Obomsawin is featured in the catalog for Imagining Indians: Native American Film and Video Festival, Scottsdale, Arizona, June 2–5, 1994.

36. Alanis Obomsawin is quoted in the official program for the 1997 Taos Talking Picture Festival, where she was honored and presented the Taos Mountain Award, 14.

37. The following short list of films illustrates the remarkable scope of Aboriginal productions: *Tikinagan* (1991), directed by Richard Cardinal (Métis); *Red Paper* (1996) and *Buffalo Bone China* (1997), directed by Dana Claxton (Lakota); *Laxwesa Wa: Strength of the River* (1995) and *'Qátuwas: People Gathering Together* (1997), directed by Barb Cranmer ('Namgis); *The Hero* (1995) and *The Gift* (1997), directed by Gary Farmer (Cayuga); *Doctor, Lawyer, Indian Chief* (1986) and *Picturing a People: George Johnston, Tlingit Photographer* (1997), directed by Carol Geddes (Tlingit); *Totem Talk* (1997), directed by Anna Frazier Henry (Sioux/Blackfeet/French); *It Starts with a Whisper* (1993), codirected by Shelly Niro (Quinte Bay Mohawk) and Anna Gronau; *Honey Moccasin* (1998), directed by Shelly Niro; *The Learning Path* (1990) and *Hands of History* (1994), discussed in chapter 5; *Forgotten Warriors* (1996) and *Today Is a Good Day* (1998), directed by Loretta Todd (Cree/Métis).

38. *StoryBoard* 2, no. 3, September 1997, a newsletter published by Pacific Islanders in Communication, Hawaii.

5. On the Road to *Smoke Signals*

1. Interview with Steve Lewis, audiotape recording, at the Imagining Indians: Native American Film and Video Festival, Scottsdale, Arizona, June 6, 1994. Interview appears also in my Ph.D. dissertation, "Film and Video Made by Native Americans: A Cultural Exploration of Film and Video Production among Native Americans" (University of New Mexico, 1996).

2. Sandra Osawa, quoted from her audiotaped panel presentation, "Can a White Man Make a Film about an Indian?" at the Imagining Indians: Native American Film and Video Festival, Scottsdale, Arizona, June 4, 1994.

3. Casey Camp Horinek, quoted from her audiotaped panel presentation, "The Life of a Native American Actor," at the Imagining Indians: Native American Film and Video Festival, June 4, 1994.

4. In 1978, the U.S. Congress sought to reverse the long history of government oppression of Native American tribal religious practices through the passage of a policy embodied in the American Indian Religious Freedom Act (AIRFA). The intent of AIRFA was to protect the religious rights of members of Indian tribes, Alaska Natives, and Native Hawaiians. Among the AIRFA policies was one to help expedite the existing federal permit system for Indian religious use of eagle feathers and assess the allocation of the surplus plant and animal parts in possession of the federal government for Native American religious use. Federal law (16 U.S.C. 668a) allows Indian religious use of eagle feathers under a U.S. Fish and Wildlife Service permit system; however, the permit sytem has had a negative impact on tribal members who have received eagle feathers ceremonially and do not have permits for the feathers. For additional information regarding AIRFA, contact the Native American Rights Fund, 1506 Broadway Street, Boulder, Colorado, 80302, (303) 447-8760, www.narf.org.

5. Alfonso Ortiz, "Indian/White Relations: A View from the Other Side of the 'Frontier,'" in *Indians in American History*, ed. Frederick W. Hoxie (Wheeling, Ill.: Harlan Davidson, 1988), 8.

6. Quotation from *Lighting the 7th Fire* (1993), dir. Sandra Johnson Osawa, Upstream Productions, Seattle, Washington.

7. Edward H. Spicer, *Cycles of Conquest* (Tucson: University of Arizona, 1976), 210–28. In the 1860s, Navajos were declared enemies of the United States, and the majority were captured and forced to walk to be imprisoned at Bosque Redondo near Fort Sumner, New Mexico, three hundred miles away from their homeland. The government held the Navajo there for four years.

8. According to the 1990 U.S. Census, 51% of the 1,959,234 Native American population resides in urban and metropolitan areas.

9. Publicity statement from Third World Newsreel (335 W. 38th St., 5th floor, New York, NY 10018).

10. According to scholar John Mohawk, professor at State University of New York, Buffalo, this was a "toll," a one-time fee. See the *New York Times* recent story "If You Believe They Paid $24, Here's a Bridge for Sale," which refers to the sale by the Indians to a Dutch man as a fable. The feature

writer Richard E. Mooney suggests, "The true story of the Manhattan purchase is an exercise in weeding the myth from fact" (*New York Times*, 28 December 1997, sec. 4, p. 2).

11. Paula Gunn Allen, *The Sacred Hoop: Recovering the Feminine in American Indian Traditions* (Boston: Beacon Press, 1986), 2.

12. John Neihardt, *Black Elk Speaks* (Lincoln: University of Nebraska Press, 1988), 67.

13. In November 1995, Loretta Todd was in New York City for the premiere of *Hands of History* at the Margaret Mead Film Festival, at which time I met with her. She explained to me that Studio D at the National Film Board of Canada is concerned with women's perspectives. She added, however, that did not make the production of *Hands of History* any easier, due to differences in experiences and worldview of white Canadian women and Aboriginal women.

14. In the film, Rena Point Bolton identifies herself only by her traditional name, a member of the Wolf Tribe from the Sto:lo Nation. In my last attempt to identify her specific tribal or band affiliation, I dialed what I thought was information in Sardis, British Columbia, at about 6:10 P.M. EST. A young woman answered the phone, and I explained that I thought I was calling information. I asked her if she knew about the Sto:lo Nation, and she told me to hold. Another young woman came to the phone and said about Rena Point Bolton, "Oh, that's my grandma." Shocked, I explained what an amazing coincidence and asked her what tribe her grandmother belonged to. She said, "Salish." I thanked her. She transferred my call to her uncle, Steven Point, Bolton's son. I repeated the reason for my call, and then I thanked him for his time and asked him for his niece's name (Joann). I am thankful for the intervention by the Great Spirit on this day, February 2, 1996.

15. Simon Ortiz, *After and Before the Lightning* (Tucson: Sun Tracks, University of Arizona, 1994), 20.

16. Georges E. Sioui, *For an Amerindian Autohistory* (Montreal: McGill-Queens University Press, 1992), 36–37.

17. Frida Kahlo (1907–1954) was a Mexican Indian artist whose paintings were autobiographical. Her life became the stage for numerous stories after her marriage to the Mexican artist Diego Rivera.

18. Theresa Harlan, "Creating a Visual History: A Question of Ownership," *Aperture* 13, no. 9 (summer 1995): 20.

Conclusion

1. Reported in the *New York Times*, "Rites of Winter," 12 February 1998, Arts section.

2. United Native American Television Broadcasting Council, contact@unat.org.

3. Jackie Bissley, "Déjà Vu in Hollywood," *Indian Country Today*, March 16–23, 1998, A8.

4. Miles Morrisseau, "Better Days on the Rez," *Aboriginal Voices* 4, no. 4 (November/December 1997): 54.

5. Yvonne Beamer interview in Beverly R. Singer, "Film and Video Made by Native Americans: A Cultural Examination of Film and Video Production by Native Americans" (Ph.D. diss., University of New Mexico, 1996), 169.

6. A festival poster was designed by Harry Fonseca, well-known for his reimagining of Coyote. Fonseca portrayed Coyote as Rudolph Valentino on location in Pueblo Indian country, complete with camels and palm trees and the iconographic Hollywood movie beacons shooting upward into a starlit sky.

7. One evening program included a reading by Ortiz after which the D. W. Griffith film *A Pueblo Legend* (1912) was to be shown with a live performance by an organist playing the original music score to the silent movie. As I made my way to the Lobo theater, I looked up at the movie marquee and read "Simon Ortiz" and, beneath his name, "A Pueblo Legend." I smiled at the compliment.

8. "Two Rivers Festival Overview," program guide. The Minneapolis American Indian Center hosted the Two Rivers Native American Film and Video Festival, October 9–13, 1991.

9. "Aboriginal Film and Video Arts Alliance Meets with Banff Centre," *Runner: Native Magazine for the Communicative Arts* (winter 1993): 24. The *Runner* has been renamed *Aboriginal Voices*.

10. Imagining Indians: Native American Film and Video Festival program catalog, Scottsdale Center for the Arts, Scottsdale, Arizona, June 2–5, 1994.

11. Panel discussion, "Intellectual Property Rights: Can Language, History, Stories, Designs, and Rituals Be Exclusively Owned?" at the Imagining Indians: Native American Film and Video Festival, June 3, 1994.

Index

BEVERLY R. SINGER is director of the Alfonso Ortiz Center for Intercultural Studies at the University of New Mexico. Her videos include *Recovery in Native America*; *A Video Book,* a video poem about her perspectives concerning Native imagery and Native cultures; and *Hózhó of Native Women.* Singer is coeditor, with Arlene Hirschfelder, of *Rising Voices: Writings by Young Native Americans.*

ROBERT WARRIOR is associate professor of English and Native American Studies at the University of Oklahoma. He is the author of *Tribal Secrets: Recovering American Indian Intellectual Traditions* (Minnesota, 1995) and, with Paul Chaat Smith, *Like a Hurricane: The Indian Movement from Alcatraz to Wounded Knee.*